Larry Kusche's

POPCORN COOKERY

ANOTHER BEST-SELLING COOKERY VOLUME FROM H.P.BOOKS

Publisher: Bill Fisher; Editor-In-Chief: Carl Shipman; Editors: Carlene Tejada, Jon Latimer; Recipes tested by: Jane Campbell, Vicki Collerette, Jane Dick, Ginnie Gipson, Sally Kusche, Peggy Pellegrini, Linda Ricketts, Kay Steinmetz, Bonnie Youree; Art Director: Josh Young; Typography: Frances Ruiz, Mary Kaye Fisher, Cindy Coatsworth, Chuck Barlean; Food Stylist: Anthony Martino; Food Photography: Don Winston, Winston-Roberts Photography.

Published by H.P. Books, P.O. Box 5367, Tucson, AZ 85703

ISBN: Softcover, 0-912656-62-X; Hardcover, 0-912656-84-0
H.P. Book Number: Softcover, 62; Hardcover, 84
Library of Congress Catalog Card Number: 77-83276 ©1977 H.P. Books. Printed in U.S.A.

What This Book Is About

This is a very unusual book. It gives you over 200 *new and delicious ways* to fix and enjoy popcorn. Some strange—some you won't believe! Be adventurous! Try these unusual recipes. You'll have fun and enjoy the delicious end results.

This book tells you how to pop popcorn. Everybody already knows how, you say? Well then, this book tells you how to pop popcorn *scientifically*. You'll get more tastycrunchy flakes of popcorn and fewer of those burned jawbreaker kernels that didn't pop. You'll get more and better popped corn for your money!

It tells you all about popcorn poppers so you become an expert popperperson. You'll learn things about electric poppers that they don't tell you on the TV commercials. You'll learn about stove-top and fireplace poppers. You'll learn the exactly correct amount of popping oil to use. You'll learn what makes popcorn pop and the scientifically correct amount of moisture that should be in each kernel. Just think what this knowledge can do for you when conversations lag. Have you heard about the Great Popcorn Slump?

This book can change your life!

There's a buyer's guide section with pictures and information on all the latest poppers. If you're going to replace that contraption you've been using, study the buyer's guide and *get the popper that's best* for you. Get one that's best for Aunt Minnie at Christmas time.

Popcorn is good for you. Imagine that! Something in this world is so good that you want to eat a bunch of it and it's actually *good for your body*. It's a diet food, too. Don't drench it with butter and it's so low in calories you can eat all you want. Make it tasty-good by following one of the snack recipes in this book that doesn't use a lot of butter. Yes. They're in here, too.

Popcorn helps little kids. Start 'em out on popcorn snacks and maybe they won't get hooked later on junk foods. Dentists like popcorn. They say, feed it to your kids.

Best of all, *popcorn is fun*. Fun to fix and fun to eat. It's a family thing that makes everybody like each other better. This book gives you fun with popcorn. And other good things, too.

Poppers

During my popper tests, I confirmed some things I'd long suspected, but never proved. Among electric poppers, those that get hotter produce better popcorn and fewer "old maids." Electric-popper temperature is mainly determined by the wattage rating. A 600-watt popper will usually make better popcorn than a 500-watt popper of the same size.

Because stove-top and fireplace non-electric poppers can reach higher temperatures, these poppers do just as well as electric units and often better. It depends on the temperature reached by the popper and the skill of the popperperson.

Agitation is sometimes very important in getting a good yield. You are expected to shake or agitate non-electric poppers so the kernels tumble around and get heated on all sides. Because agitation distributes the heat, oil is not always needed in non-electric poppers. Oil is used instead of agitation in electric poppers to distribute the heat to all sides of the kernels. Shaking an electric popper with boiling oil inside *is dangerous* and electric-popper manufacturers *do not recommend shaking* the popper.

Commercial electric poppers and at least one home-type electric popper have a motor-driven stirrer to agitate the popcorn automatically without anybody doing any shaking. These are usually used with oil also, and they make very good popcorn.

Millions of families use electric poppers with complete satisfaction and enjoy delicious popcorn. They are convenient and require no special skill to use. They don't require a lot of attention—but they require some. They operate at a *good* popping temperature.

A lot of other people use an old pan on top of the kitchen stove. This can make popcorn as good, or better than an electric popper, but the stove temperature must be right. Too cold or too hot and the popcorn is inferior. Stove-top popping requires constant attention from the popperperson and constant agitation.

POPPING WITHOUT A POPPER

A frying pan, deep skillet or pressure cooker can be used to pop popcorn. Aluminum pans work best, but other types can be used. Slightly less heat is needed when using a stainless-steel pan. Some electric skillets also make good poppers. Set the thermostat to 425°F (218°C) or 450°F (232°C) and use like a non-electric popper.

These should be shaken well once the popping begins. If the pan is too heavy or awkward to shake, many kernels will fail to pop or will burn. If you have this trouble with your pan, try reducing the heat slightly. It is easier to lift some electric skillets to shake them than to slide them back and forth. Be *very careful* not to spill the oil!

When you pop popcorn cover the utensil. A tight-fitting cover should have a steam vent. If you use aluminum foil for a cover, puncture the foil in 2 or 3 places to allow the steam to escape.

Use the same amount of oil and popcorn as directed for the same size non-electric popper in the discussion that follows. Popping time may be less than 4 minutes.

NON-ELECTRIC POPPERS

If you have not used a non-electric popper before, you may be surprised by the rapidity and violence of the popping. It may all be over before you realize it. The time from first pop to last may be as little as 30 seconds. Anything over 1 minute is slow and may cause scorching.

The most common mistake is to hold a non-electric popper over the heat too long because it doesn't seem the corn could have popped that fast. It can. Move the popper away from the heat 10 seconds *before* the anticipated end of popping. Continue shaking until popping stops, then dump the popcorn into a bowl.

Non-electric poppers work extremely well. Their primary disadvantage is that most of them are small.

Nº 2 Wagon

One of the early popcorn machines was this Cretors Number 2 Wagon.

This old-time popcorn wagon adds old-fashioned enjoyment to Opryland U.S.A.® in Nashville, Tennessee.

TIPS FOR USING NON-ELECTRIC POPPERS

Plan ahead. Begin melting the butter well before you start the popping because it takes much longer. Have the salt and other garnishes at hand. Make sure you have a large bowl nearby for the popcorn and a place picked out for setting the hot popper after it is emptied. A cool stove burner is a good place. Do not run water on a hot popper to cool it because it may warp.

Warn children to stand back, especially when popping ends. They want to hover over the popper to watch the action. The pan gets very hot and you will have to move fast once the popping stops.

Best results are obtained by using high heat.

Popping time can be cut in half by going from next-to-high to high heat on an electric stove, but when using a gas stove, do not let the flames go up the side of the popper.

Proper shaking or stirring, prompt removal from heat, and prompt pouring from the popper are necessary to avoid scorching. Excessive shaking and stirring at the beginning can retard popping, but vigorous shaking or stirring is necessary near the end.

When popping oil is used, it is not necessary to shake or stir until the popping starts. When no oil is used, begin shaking or stirring a little before the popping starts. Using oil lengthens popping time about a minute.

ELECTRIC-POPPER DIFFERENCES

The difference between *automatic* and *non-automatic* electric poppers is important.

Automatic electric poppers have a built-in thermostat to turn off the electric power to the heating element when the heating surface reaches about 480°F (249°C). The power remains off until the temperature drops to about 360°F (182°C). Then the thermostat turns the power on again and the cycle repeats. After the first cycle, complete cycles usually take 4 to 6 minutes. Some thermostats click loudly each time they switch on or off. Automatic poppers *do not shut off completely*. All come back on unless the cord is unplugged.

Non-automatic electric poppers don't have a thermostat. When plugged in, they start getting hot. They keep getting hotter until finally they get as hot as they possibly can. If left plugged in, they will stay very hot. Unplug and pour the popcorn out as soon as popping is completed.

HEATING POWER (WATTAGE)

The most important thing about a popper is how hot it gets. Hotter poppers pop more kernels and produce larger pieces. As a rule, the best popper pops the popcorn in the shortest time.

A 500-watt popper is usually adequate only if the popper has less than a 4-quart capacity. One with 600 or more watts will pop faster and cause less scorching because the popcorn will be in contact with heat for less time.

HEATING-SURFACE DESIGN

Popping is a violent explosion. The popping kernel jumps away from the heating surface, scattering other kernels. In theory, a surface which slants toward the heated center will help these scattered kernels slide back to the heating surface and give them another chance to pop. In practice, I found a slanted surface may produce a few less "old maids" or "grannies"—kernels which don't pop—but it is relatively unimportant compared to the temperature reached by the heating surface.

OIL LINE

Many electric poppers with slanted bottoms have an oil line on their heating surfaces. Pour oil into the popper until it reaches the line. This should be the correct amount for popping. If you check with a measuring cup, it should be about 1/3 the recommended volume of popcorn kernels.

BUTTER DISPENSERS

Automatic butter dispensers are designed to make popping easier by saving you the trouble of heating butter in a separate pan. I found that choosing the time for adding butter is absolutely crucial for proper distribution. If you put butter in the dispenser too soon, it will melt and drop into the oil and lower its temperature, thereby reducing popcorn quality. If the butter is put in too late, not all of it will melt. Butter that does melt tends to saturate the popcorn directly beneath the dispenser and leave the rest untouched.

Best popcorn results from not using the butter dispenser. Melt the butter in a separate pan and drizzle it over the popped popcorn. The recipes in this book do not require a butter dispenser.

Incidentally, check that the butter-dispenser lid is securely attached to the popper cover before turning the popper over to remove the popped corn.

COVERS

The weakest part of an electric popper is the plastic cover. It can crack or warp with careless handling. It can be scratched if you use the wrong materials to clean it. Follow the maker's directions or those in the Buyer's Guide.

SIGNAL LIGHT

A signal light is usually the glow of the heating element seen through an opening in the base. It is supposed to tell you when popping is finished by going out. All it really says is that the thermostat has sensed maximum temperature and turned off power to the heating element. Signal lights are not an accurate indicator of when popping is finished. The best way to tell when popping is over is by listening.

CORD

Cord should be 2- to 3-feet long and detachable from the popper. Longer cords are undesirable because they tangle and may become a safety hazard. All cords should carry the Underwriter's Laboratories Inc.® seal.

USING EXTENSION CORDS

Extension cords increase the danger of accidentally tripping or tangling. If you *must* use an extension cord, make sure the electrical rating of the cord is at least as great as the rating of the appliance. Arrange the cord so it is out of the way of children.

CLEANING ELECTRIC POPPERS

Each of the popper descriptions in the Buyer's Guide contains directions for cleaning. In general, a few simple rules should be followed.

1. Allow the popper to cool completely before cleaning.

2. Never immerse the popcorn base. None of those tested are waterproof, and the danger of short-circuiting the popper, or getting a shock, is very high if water seeps into the electrical system. Water can also cause electrical malfunctions.

3. Don't scour the plastic or non-stick coatings with abrasive cleansers or scouring pads.

Your popper should not need any maintenance other than cleaning.

REMOVING STAINS FROM THE NON-STICK SURFACE

Some oil and butter may settle into the porous finish of the base after continued use. This residue may carbonize when the base is reheated and cause the base to discolor. These stains can be removed with a soft cloth saturated with lemon juice or vinegar.

Several manufacturers recommend pouring a mixture of 1 cup boiling water, 2 tablespoons baking soda, and 1/2 cup liquid bleach into the popper base. This mix is boiled in the heated popper for 10 minutes, or until the stains disappear. This may cause the color of the non-stick surface to change, but it will not affect the performance of the popper.

Some manufacturers recommend *against* cleaning the surface with bleach. Check the instructions before proceeding.

ABUSE TEST

Electric poppers shown in this book were subjected to an abuse test. I allowed the loaded popper to remain plugged in for periods of up to 12 hours. The popper passed the test if after 3 or more hours there was no melting or warping of the base and cover, there was no smoke or strong smell and the popper did not create a fire danger by itself or to the area around it. All automatic poppers passed this part of the test.

I then cleaned the automatic poppers and checked to see if they would still make good popcorn. They did.

Several poppers were tested empty. Although their tops became hotter than when they were loaded, there was no fire hazard.

Poppers which had problems were non-automatic units which the manufacturer warns should be watched. That goes for automatics, too. All poppers should be carefully watched and unplugged when popping stops.

Buyer's Guide

NON-ELECTRIC WITH STIRRER

ALADDIN NO-SHAKE CORN POPPER

This all-aluminum pan has plastic handles on the side and lid. A stirring wire is attached to the underside of the lid. When the popcorn begins to pop, rotate the cover to stir the popcorn. Both pan and lid get very hot so empty the popcorn as soon as the popping stops to prevent scorching. Be careful not to touch the hot pan or lid. Press down slightly as you turn the lid to prevent the exploding popcorn from lifting it. Once it has lifted, it is difficult to press it back down without crushing some of the popped corn and stopping rotation. Be especially careful not to overload the popper. Too many kernels result in overflows or crushed popcorn. If the lid refuses to turn, try turning it in the opposite directions.

You can make excellent popcorn with this popper if the directions are followed. Very few kernels are left unpopped.

Capacity—3 quarts.

Recommended Quantities—Oil: 1/8 inch in bottom of pan, approximately 1/3 cup. Popcorn: 1/3 cup to 1/2 cup. With high-volume popcorn use no more than 1/4 cup. Salt: One teaspoon can be added if desired.

Popping Time—4 to 5 minutes over high heat.

Clean Up—After the pan and lid cool, wash them with hot water and soap, or in an automatic dishwasher. Scouring may be necessary to remove stains.

NON-ELECTRIC WITH STIRRER

BRINKMAN POPALL POPPER

This popper is an aluminum pail with a crank to stir the popcorn as it pops. It makes excellent popcorn and can make recipes that cannot be duplicated with any other machine. You can make sugared popcorn, for example, by putting 1/2 cup of sugar in with the kernels. Also, very few old maids occur with this popper. Popping is fast with this machine. Use high heat. When popping starts, slowly turn the crank to stir the popcorn. If you don't use oil, reduce the heat slightly and begin cranking as soon as you put the popper on. The pail becomes very hot during cooking, but the wooden handles protect your hands adequately.

Popcorn pops larger in this machine than in most others, and there is a danger of overloading the machine. If a full load stops the crank from turning, turn it in the opposite direction. This popper can also be used on a glass-top stove because it is not moved back and forth and will not scratch the heating surface.

Capacity—4 quarts.

Recommended Quantities—Oil: 3 tablespoons. Popcorn: 1/2 cup. With high-expansion popcorn use 1/3 cup.

Popping Time—3-1/2 minutes from the time the heat is turned on for electric stoves, faster over an open fire.

Clean Up—Separate the lid and the pail and wash them with soap and water or in an automatic dishwasher. Occasional scouring may be necessary to remove stains from the pail. If desired, simply wipe the parts clean with a cloth, allowing the oil to season the popper.

Long Handle Model—Has a 16-1/2-inch-long handle and is designed for use in a fireplace or over a campfire.

Popcorn Institute Seal of Approval

NON-ELECTRIC

BROMWELL CORNPOPPER

These poppers are slightly different versions of the basic Cornpopper. They are made of steel and have wooden handles. They can be used on a grill, stove, fireplace or campfire with or without oil. They make excellent popcorn extremely fast. When popping is finished, quickly remove the popper from the heat and turn it over to keep the popped popcorn from being burnt by the hot bottom of the pan.

Besides popping popcorn, these pans can be used for frying and for warming rolls.

Capacity—Almost 3 quarts.

Recommended Quantities—Oil: Zero to 1/4 cup. Popcorn: 1/4 to 1/3 cup.

Popping Time—2 to 3 minutes from placing popper over high heat.

Clean Up—Do not wash with water after use; wipe clean with a paper towel. Popper can also be coated with a light covering of vegetable oil.

Outdoor Cornpopper—Sides and bottom of the outdoor model are perforated, making it ideal for fast popping on a grill, fireplace, or campfire. Can be used on a stove, but requires careful cleaning afterwards. Handle is 14-1/2-inches long.

Old-Fashioned Corn Popper—Same as the Cornpopper except with a black pan and a red, yellow or avocado lid.

Easy Store Corn Popper—Comes with a 2-piece, removable handle 3 inches longer than the basic model. Handle can be stored inside the pan when popper is not in use.

Cook 'N Pop™ Multipurpose Cooker Kit—Handle like the Easy Store; comes with an extra-long-tine fork and a steak grill. All store inside the pan to make a compact kit to take on outings. Fork can be attached to the handle for cooking hotdogs, shish-kebabs or marshmallows over an open fire.

HAMILTON BEACH BUTTER-UP® SELF-BUTTERING CORN POPPER—Model 500G

Aluminum base has a heating surface coated with a non-stick material. Base and the 2-1/2-foot detachable cord are listed with Underwriter's Laboratory, Inc.® This automatic popper has an internal thermostat.

The yellow-plastic cover can be used as a bowl after popping. It has a built-in butter dispenser with a 3-1/2-inch plastic cover which is similar to the kind found on items in grocery stores. Punch holes in the lid first.

A cup in the slanted bottom is filled with popcorn and oil is added until it is level with the corn. Metal base and the rim around it become very hot during popping, but the handles remain cool and their design helps prevent the metal from being touched accidentally.

Melted butter from the dispenser seems to concentrate in the center of the popcorn.

A few kernels may scorch during popping, and an above average number of unpopped kernals are left after popping.

The unit is easy to turn over after popping. Care should be taken to avoid touching the hot metal rim and base. The popper can be left plugged in after popping as long as 5 minutes without damaging the popcorn. After 10 minutes the bottom layer of popcorn scorches.

Capacity—4 quarts.
Power—600 watts.
Thermostat—Yes.
Recommended Quantities—Oil: 1/4 cup. Popcorn: 2/3 cup. Only 1/2 cup of high-expansion popcorn should be used. Butter: 2 tablespoons cut in pieces.
Popping Time—7 minutes.
Abuse Test—Passed.
Clean Up—Wash cover with hot water and soap or in a dishwasher. Wipe heating surface with a damp cloth. Do not immerse the base.
Popcorn Institute Seal of Approval.

HAMILTON BEACH BUTTER-UP® SELF-BUTTERING CORN POPPER—Model 507

This popper is a variation of the Model 500G. Its heating surface is polished aluminum instead of non-stick material. Its butter dispenser has a larger top than 500G, but dispenses butter the same way.
Clean Up—Cover can washed with hot water and soap or in a dishwasher. The heating surface should be wiped thoroughly with a damp cloth. A soap-filled steel-wool pad can be used to remove stubborn stains. Do not immerse this popper.

MIRRO-MATIC POP 'N' SERVE SELF-BUTTERING CORN POPPER

Plastic base has a narrow metal rim. Heating surface is covered with Teflon II®. Smokey-grey Lexan® plastic cover contains a butter dispenser. This automatic popper has an internal thermostat. Base and 30-inch detachable cord are listed with Underwriter's Laboratory, Inc.®

Performs well when the manufacturer's instruction are followed. Butter dispenser works better than average. Plastic base does not get hot during popping, but the rim does. Be especially careful not to touch the rim when turning the unit over after popping.

No scorching occurs if directions are followed. If the popper is left plugged in, there will be some scorching during the first 2 minutes after popping ceases. After 10 minutes the center of the bottom layer burns, but the remainder of the popcorn is edible.

Capacity—4 quarts.
Power—600 watts.
Thermostat—Yes.
Recommended Quantities—Oil: 5 tablespoons. Popcorn: 2/3 cup. Use only 1/2 cup of high-expansion popcorn.
Popping Time—7 to 8 minutes.
Abuse Test—Passed.
Clean Up—Cover, but not butter-dispenser lid, may be washed in a dishwasher or with hot water and soap. Wash heating surface with hot water and soap, but do not immerse the base.
Popcorn Institute Seal of Approval.

MIRRO SUPER-SPEED CORN POPPER

Despite its low power, this unit works as well as many poppers with much higher wattage. Cover and the base are aluminum with plastic handles and legs. Automatic and has an internal thermostat and a signal light. Base and 33-inch detachable cord are listed with Underwriter's Laboratory, Inc.® There is no butter dispenser.

This popper pops well when the directions are followed, but the exterior gets hot enough to cause burns. The surface beneath the popper does not heat up, and the handles remain adequately cool.

If left plugged in, no scorching occurs during the first 5 minutes after popping has stopped. An average amount of unpopped kernels is left behind after popping.

Capacity—3 quarts.
Power—490 watts.
Thermostat—Yes.
Recommended Quantities—Oil: 3 tablespoons. Popcorn: 1/2 cup.
Popping Time—7 to 9 minutes.
Abuse Test—Passed.
Clean Up—Cover may be placed in an automatic washer. Use a soap-filled steel-wool pad to scour off grease marks. Rinse and dry thoroughly. Base can be washed with soap and water, but should not be immersed. If oil accumulates on the outside, remove it with metal polish. Heavier deposits can be removed with a scouring pad.
Popcorn Institute Seal of Approval.

MUNSEY BUTTER-MATIC CORN POPPER

This popper comes with 4 plastic serving bowls. Cover is grey plastic and has a butter dispenser. The dispenser covers a very small area and melting butter in another pan is recommended. The dispenser is automatic; the popper is not.

The base is painted aluminum and has a removable aluminum pan that lifts off the heating element for easy cleaning. The heating element is tubular, similar to those on kitchen ranges. Both the base and the 24-inch detachable cord are listed with Underwriter's Laboratory, Inc.®

Using the manufacturer's recommended ingredients produced unacceptable popcorn. Large numbers of kernels were left unpopped, some corn was scorched, and popping time stretched beyond 10 minutes. Reducing the ingredients to the quantities listed below gave better results. Slight scorching still occurred at the end of popping.

Base and metal legs become very hot during popping and the surface beneath the popper should be protected. The plastic handles remain cool.

Capacity—4 quarts.

Power—525 watts.

Thermostat—None.

Author's Recommended Quantities—Oil: 3 tablespoons. Popcorn: 1/2 cup.

Popping Time—10 minutes.

Abuse Test—Smoke from burning popcorn appeared after 15 minutes. The popper passed the rest of the test.

Clean Up—The cover should be washed with soap and water and a soft cloth. The removable popping bowl can be washed in an automatic dishwasher. Do not immerse the heating unit.

MUNSEY CORN POPPER

The top of this non-automatic popper is made of glass. The base is painted aluminum and has two parts: an aluminum pan which can be lifted off and cleaned separately, and a tubular heating element like those on kitchen ranges. Both base and 24-inch detachable cord are listed with Underwriter's Laboratory, Inc.® Four plastic serving bowls are included.

Following the manufacturer's directions for this popper does not produce acceptable popcorn. By reducing the amounts of ingredients to those recommended below, the results are better, but not as good as other poppers tested.

Popping time is very long and the outside of this popper becomes extremely hot during popping. The metal legs conduct heat and the surface beneath the popper should be protected.

Capacity—3 quarts.

Power—525 watts.

Thermostat—None.

Author's Recommended Quantities—Oil: 3 tablespoons. Popcorn: 1/2 cup.

Popping Time—10 minutes.

Abuse Test—Dark smoke from burning popcorn appeared after 15 minutes. This continued until the popper was unplugged. The popper passed the rest of the abuse test.

Clean Up—The cover and the removable popping bowl can be washed in an automatic dishwasher. The heating element should not be immersed.

PRESTO AUTOMATIC-BUTTERING CORN POPPER

This automatic popper has an internal thermostat. The signal light is actually the glow of the heating element. Outside is painted aluminum. Heating surface slants steeply toward the center. It is coated with a non-stick material called *Presto Hard Surface*.

Base and detachable 36-inch cord are listed with Underwriter's Laboratory, Inc.®

The yellow Lexan® plastic lid can be used as a bowl. A butter dispenser in the lid has a separate Lexan® top that screws into the underside. The dispenser works as well as any of the others tested. The surface beneath this popper becomes very warm during popping. Handles connected to the base become uncomfortably warm; those on the lid remain cool. The entire unit is easy to turn over to remove the popped corn, but take special care not to touch the metal next to the handles or the handles themselves when removing the base.

Despite its wattage, this popper scorches very few pieces, even when left on 10 minutes after popping is complete. It leaves only a moderate amount of unpopped kernels. Works well if the directions are followed.

Capacity—4 quarts.

Power—650 watts.

Thermostat—Yes.

Recommended Quantities—Oil: 3/4 cup. Popcorn: 1/2 cup. Butter: 1 to 2 tablespoons.

Popping Time—Under 7 minutes.

Abuse Test—Passed.

Clean Up—Use hot water and soap on lid and heating surface, but do not immerse the base. Do not wash in an automatic dishwasher.

REGAL WARE POLY POP™ BUTTERCUP POPCORN POPPER

The outside of this popper is plastic and the cover is smoke-tinted Lexan® plastic. The flat heating surface is coated with Teflon II®. The automatic unit has an internal thermostat. Base and 30-inch detachable cord are listed with Underwriter's Laboratory, Inc.®

A butter dispenser on the cover has a 4-inch plastic lid similar to those found on many grocery products. If refrigerated butter is placed in the dispenser, it will not melt by the time popping is completed. Using butter at room temperature requires taking it out of the refrigerator 5 to 10 minutes before popping. Most of the melted butter falls on the center of the corn, and much of the corn is not buttered.

This popper pops well. The plastic becomes very hot during popping. The small handles become very warm and the popper must be handled carefully when it is turned over to empty the popcorn. Be especially careful when lifting the base off the cover because the narrow handles may cause you to touch the hot plastic. The top also gets hot, but this helps to keep the popped popcorn warm when it is used as a bowl.

This popper does not scorch the popcorn even if it is left plugged in for an hour after popping has stopped.

Capacity—4 quarts.
Power—650 watts.
Thermostat—Yes.
Recommended Quantities—Oil: 3 tablespoons. Popcorn: 1/3 to 1/2 cup. Butter: 2 tablespoons at room temperature.
Popping Time—5 to 6 minutes.
Abuse Test—Passed.
Clean Up—Wash lid in soap and hot water, do not use abrasives. Clean heating surface with a soapy sponge or dishcloth, wipe with a damp cloth and dry. Wipe the plastic surfaces of the base with a damp cloth. Do not immerse the base. Do not wash in an automatic dishwasher. Popcorn Institute Seal of Approval.

RELIABLE FLAVO-RITE™ AUTOMATIC TEFLON®-LINED ELECTRIC CORN POPPER WITH BUTTERCUP
MONTGOMERY WARD AUTOMATIC TEFLON®-LINED ELECTRIC CORN POPPER WITH BUTTERCUP

Outside of base is plastic; cover is yellow-orange plastic. Heating surface is moderately slanted and Teflon®-coated. Butter dispenser in cover has a 4-inch plastic top and distributes butter well. Base and 36-inch detachable cord are listed with Underwriter's Laboratory, Inc.®

Base and the handles stay reasonably cool during popping. Popper is easy to turn over and base easily removed when popping is completed.

There is some scorching at the end of the popping cycle. Unplug the popper and turn it over promptly. If left plugged in more than 5 minutes after popping stops, most of the bottom layer scorches. Remaining popcorn is edible. Leaves an average amount of kernels unpopped.

Capacity—4 quarts.
Power—500 watts.
Thermostat—Yes.
Recommended Quantities—Oil: 1/2 cup. Popcorn: 1/2 cup. Butter: 2 or 3 tablespoons cut into 4 pieces.
Popping Time—7-1/2 to 8-1/2 minutes.
Abuse Test—Passed.
Clean Up—Cover can be washed in a dishwasher. Use hot water and soap on the heating surface, but be careful not to let the water enter the electrical area. Do not immerse the base.

SUNBEAM® THE GREAT AMERICAN POPCORN MACHINE™

This decorative model of an old-fashioned popcorn wagon comes with 4 wheels that must be attached to provide clearance so the surface beneath the popper won't heat up.

The cover is light-yellow plastic. The base is plastic-covered and the heating surface is coated with Teflon II®. It has an internal thermostat. Base and 36-inch detachable cord are listed with Underwriter's Laboratory, Inc.®

A butter dispenser built into the cover has a 7-1/2 by 3-1/2-inch plastic lid specially designed for this popper. Butter distribution equals other poppers.

This popper does a fair job of popping if the directions are followed. Hot pads are recommended for protection when turning the unit over to empty the popcorn. The whole popper becomes very hot.

This popper may scorch a few pieces of corn if it is not unplugged and emptied immediately after popping stops. After 5 minutes, the bottom layer of popcorn scorches.

Capacity—4 quarts.
Power—650 watts.
Thermostat—Yes.
Recommended Quantities—Oil: 3 tablespoons. Popcorn: 1/2 to 2/3 cups. Butter: 1 to 2 tablespoons.
Popping Time—6 minutes.
Abuse Test—Passed.
Clean Up—Cover should be washed with warm water and soap, but not in a dishwasher. The heating surface should be wiped with a damp cloth. Soap can be used if necessary, but be sure to remove the soap film. Do not use scouring pads on any part of this popper. Do not immerse the base.

NON-ELECTRIC

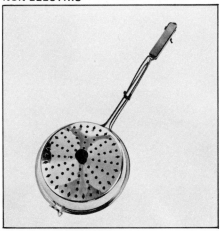

TEMPLET POPPER GRILL

This popper is extremely fast when used over high heat on a stove or campfire. Once popping begins, the popper must be shaken continuously. Some oil spatters out of the holes in the lid during popping. Take care to hold the handle level as the rounded bottom of the pan causes it to tilt. Remove the popcorn quickly when the popping has finished. This popper makes excellent popcorn when the directions are followed.

Steel pan has a removable brass lid. With the lid on, the grill can be used for grilling sandwiches and baking potatoes. Without the lid, it becomes a frying pan.

Capacity—2 quarts.

Recommended Quantities—Oil: 3 tablespoons. Popcorn: 1/3 cup.

Popping Time—3 minutes.

Clean Up—Can be washed with hot water and soap or in an automatic dishwasher.

APPROVED POPCORN POPPERS

The Popcorn Institute's Seal of Approval™ means the popper has been tested for safety, ease of operation and consistent production of quality popcorn. The machine must perform as advertised. The popcorn it produces is even tested for crispness and flavor.

The Seal of Approval is not a warranty. It is given to individual models rather than to a manufacturer's entire line. The seal usually appears on the carton or the directions packed with the popper. Poppers awarded the seal should make crisp and tender popcorn if proper procedures and quality ingredients are used.

AUTOMATIC ELECTRIC

TOASTMASTER® SELF-BUTTERING CORN POPPER

This automatic popper has an internal thermostat. The yellow-plastic cover contains a butter dispenser with a 4-inch top. The heating surface is polished aluminum and the outside of the base is painted aluminum. Base and 24-inch detachable cord are listed with Underwriter's Laboratory, Inc.®

When pouring in the oil, tilt the popper in various directions to spread it or you may add too much.

The metal base becomes very hot during popping, but the handles remain cool. After popping, the unit can be turned over easily to convert the top to a bowl. Be careful to avoid touching the metal.

Directions say, put the butter in the dispenser before the cord is plugged in. This caused the butter to melt before the popcorn started popping. Butter dripped into the popping oil and lowered its temperature, slowing the popping and extending it beyond 10 minutes. Some scorching occurred and a large number of kernels remained unpopped. Adding butter when the first kernel popped did not improve these results. This popper works better when no butter is used in the dispenser. No scorching occurs, but a large number of kernels remain unpopped.

Capacity—4 quarts.

Power—500 watts.

Thermostat—Yes.

Recommended Quantities—Oil: 1/3 cup. Popcorn: 2/3 cup. Butter: Manufacturer suggests 2 tablespoons cut in 3 pieces.

Popping Time—8 to 10 minutes.

Abuse Test—Passed.

Clean Up—After each use, wash the cover, butter dispenser and heating surface with hot water and soap, and rinse them thoroughly with hot water. Do not immerse the base. Do not wash in an automatic dishwasher.

AUTOMATIC ELECTRIC

WEAR-EVER PARTY POPPER

Cover is yellow-orange Lexan® plastic and the base is covered with plastic. Flat heating surface is coated with white Telfon II®. This automatic popper has an internal thermostat. Base and 36-inch detachable cord are listed with Underwriter's Laboratory, Inc.®

Butter dispenser in cover has a hinged top. Directions specify using room-temperature butter which requires taking it from the refrigerator 5 or 10 minutes before popping. Dispenser distributes butter as well as any of the others tested.

Base becomes very warm during popping, but not hot enough to cause burns. Handles do not get hot, which makes this popper easy to turn over to detach the cover. The surface beneath the popper does become warm.

Leaves a higher number of kernels unpopped than most of the other poppers tested. A few pieces may scorch, even when the popper is unplugged and emptied promptly. If left plugged in an additional 5 minutes, the bottom layer of popcorn scorches. After 10 minutes the top of the popcorn begins to turn brown.

Capacity—4 quarts.

Power—600 watts.

Thermostat—Yes.

Recommended Quantities—Oil: 1/4 cup. Popcorn: 2/3 cup. Butter: 1 to 3 tablespoons, each divided into 4 equal parts.

Abuse Test—Passed.

Clean Up—Cover and base can be washed with warm water and soap, but do not immerse the base or allow the electrical area to get wet. Do not wash in an automatic dishwasher.

AUTOMATIC ELECTRIC

NON-AUTOMATIC ELECTRIC

AUTOMATIC ELECTRIC WITH STIRRER

WEST BEND® BUTTER-MATIC® CORN POPPER and J.C. PENNEY SELF-BUTTERING CORN POPPER

Cover is made of yellow-orange Lexan® plastic and the base is plastic covered. Heating surface is coated with a non-stick material and slants slightly to a flat center. Popper is automatic with an internal thermostat. Base and 30-inch detachable cord are listed with Underwriter's Laboratory, Inc.®

Butter dispenser in the cover distributes butter better than most of those tested. It has a 4-inch plastic top like those found on various products in grocery stores.

Neither the base nor the handles get too hot to touch during popping. Popper is easy to turn over and there is no problem with removing the base. Does not scorch popcorn during normal popping, but will if not unplugged and emptied promptly. After 5 minutes, most of the bottom layer of popcorn scorches. After 10 minutes, the bottom layer is thoroughly burned and the rest of the popcorn tastes burned.

Capacity—4 quarts.

Power—525 watts.

Thermostat—Yes.

Recommended Quantities—Oil: 1/4 cup. Popcorn 2/3 cup. Butter: 3 tablespoons cut into 4 equal pieces.

Popping Time—8 to 10 minutes.

Abuse Test—Passed.

Clean Up—Cover and base can be washed with hot water and soap. Do not wash in an automatic dishwasher. Do not immerse the base.

WEST BEND® SELF-BUTTERING ELECTRIC CORN POPPER

This aluminum popper has a clear Lexan® plastic cover and a slanted aluminum heating surface. Both the popper and the 30-inch detachable cord are listed with Underwriter's Laboratory, Inc.®

A butter dispenser, located at the top of the cover, distributes the butter moderately well. Put the butter in at the proper time or it will melt before popping is underway.

This unit works well if the instructions are followed. Base becomes too hot to touch during operation, but the handle remains cool. The surface on which the popper stands does not heat up.

Popper should be unplugged and the popcorn poured out as soon as the popping stops. As the manufacturer carefully points out, this popper is not automatic. It will continue to produce high heat as long as it is plugged in.

Capacity—4 quarts.

Power—525 watts.

Thermostat—None.

Recommended Quantities—Oil: 1/4 cup. Popcorn: 1/2 cup (heaping). Butter: 3 tablespoons cut into 4 equal portions.

Popping Time—7 to 9 minutes.

Abuse Test—Because this popper is not automatic, it will burn popcorn if left plugged in. After 4 hours of steady heat, the cover melted and produced a choking black smoke. However, after 5-1/2 hours, there seemed to be no risk of fire and the test was stopped. The machine was cleaned after the abuse test and a new cover was obtained. The popper then made as good popcorn as ever.

Clean Up—Cover can be washed with soap and water. Base should not be immersed, but the inside can be cleaned with soap and water.

WEST BEND® STIR CRAZY™ CORN POPPER

The stirring rod and the high wattage make this automatic popper unique. The rod stirs the popcorn as it pops causing the kernels to heat evenly and keeping the popped corn from scorching. This popper is very fast and leaves almost no unpopped kernels. This popper makes excellent popcorn.

The cover is made of yellow plastic and has a butter dispenser. Because of the stirring, butter is distributed better than with any dispenser tested. However, since high heat causes butter to lose much of its flavor, melting the butter separately is still recommended.

The base is covered with plastic and the heating surface is coated with a non-stick surface. The base and the 30-inch detachable cord are listed with Underwriter's Laboratory, Inc.®

During popping neither the base nor the handle become too hot to touch. This popper will not scorch popcorn even when left running for 30 minutes beyond completion of popping.

Capacity—Up to 6 quarts.

Power—1000 watts.

Thermostat—Yes.

Recommended Quantities—For 2 quarts - Oil: 1 tablespoon. Popcorn: 1/3 cup. Butter: 1 tablespoon. For 4 quarts - Oil: 2 tablespoons. Popcorn: 2/3 cup. Butter: 2 tablespoons. For 6 quarts - Oil: 3 tablespoons. Popcorn: 1 cup. Butter: 3 tablespoons.

Popping Time—4 minutes for 4 quarts, 5 minutes for 6 quarts.

Abuse Test—Passed.

Clean Up—No part should be washed in a dishwasher. The cover and base should be washed with soap and water using a soft cloth. Do not immerse the base. Remove the rod for cleaning by unscrewing the center knob. Wash with hot water and soap.

Popcorn Institute Seal of Approval

CHILDREN AND POPPERS

Popcorn popping is fun to watch. Children are attracted to poppers more than any other appliance. Children should use poppers only under the strictest supervision.

POPCORN POPPER SAFETY RULES

Poppers can cause serious injury if not handled properly. Popcorn doesn't begin to pop until the temperature reaches 300°F (149°C), and the temperature can go as high as 500°F (260°C).

When using an electric popper observe basic precautions:

1. Read *all* the manufacturer's instructions.

2. Don't allow the cord or base near water or other liquids.

3. Attach the cord to the popper first, then plug into the outlet. When disconnecting, remove from the outlet first.

4. Don't leave a popper plugged in. Unplug it as soon as popping stops.

5. Protect the surface under the popper with a heat-resistant pad if necessary. Don't move a popper containing hot oil.

6. Don't lift the lid while popcorn is popping. When popping stops, lift the edge away from your face first to avoid the hot vapor.

7. Don't use a popper for anything other than popping corn.

How To Pop Popcorn

POPPING WITH BUTTER

Most instructions tell you not to use butter as a popping oil because it will smoke and burn before the corn pops. I used butter as a popping oil in both electric and non-electric poppers and it didn't smoke or burn. However, the flavor was weak compared to butter melted separately and poured over the popped corn. Use butter or margarine as a popping oil only if nothing else is available. Use cooking oil or popping oil if you have some. Some people use a mixture of half butter and half oil for popping, but I think the flavor suffers.

POPPING OIL

To make popcorn kernels pop, they must be heated all over, not just on one side. Popping oil surrounds the kernels and distributes heat to all sides.

In a popper that is shaken, the kernels are heated on all sides because they are rotated. If the popper is shaken properly and removed promptly from the heat, popping oil isn't necessary. In an electric popper, oil takes the place of the shaking and distributes the heat.

Poppers with stirring rods normally need popping oil. Without oil, or shaking, most kernels will not pop.

You can use any cooking oil to pop popcorn, so long as it doesn't burn or smoke below 500°F (260°C). The most commonly used popping oils are peanut, corn, vegetable and coconut: The latter is often used by theaters and concessionaires. There are also oils made especially for popping corn, some with an artificial butter flavor.

FLAVORED OILS

If you like a subtle flavor of onion or garlic, pour the required amount of popping oil into a small bowl several hours before popping popcorn and add chopped onion or garlic. Cover and let the mixture stand until you are ready to pop the popcorn. Remove the pieces of onion or garlic and use the oil as you normally would. The taste is a delicious variation.

Popcorn popped in bacon drippings has a distinctive flavor. Popcorn can also be popped in hamburger or sausage drippings which is handy on camping trips. Surprisingly, the flavor of popped corn is only slightly influenced by the popping oil until salt is added. Heat drives out much of the flavor, but salt brings some of it back.

SHOULD SALT BE ADDED TO THE POPPING OIL?

Adding salt to the popping oil may make the popped popcorn tough or increase the popping time. Placing salt in the oil gives it a slightly different flavor, apparently because the salt gets spread more uniformly than when it comes from a shaker. Salt may cause eventual deterioration of the heating surface. I don't put salt in the oil.

PRE-HEATING THE OIL

Some directions call for letting the oil get hot, then placing 2 or 3 test kernels in it and waiting until they pop before adding the remaining kernels.

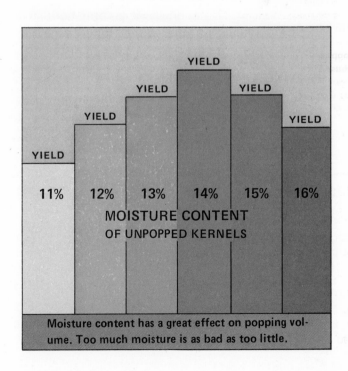

Moisture content has a great effect on popping volume. Too much moisture is as bad as too little.

Others call for spacing all the kernels in the oil at the start. I found no discernible difference between the two methods, either in volume or in taste. Because heating the oil and using test kernels adds another step, I suggest that you put all the kernels in the oil at the start.

HOW TO MEASURE THE OIL AND POPCORN

For many years I just "eye-balled" it when making popcorn. Three or four glugs of oil and a fistful of kernels did the job. Then one day I followed the directions on the label. The yield almost doubled for what appeared to be the same amount of kernels.

Popping directions vary from one brand of popcorn to another, but they are fairly consistent. Popper manufacturers want the popper to look good, so they recommend using more popcorn than the popcorn processors suggest. Most popper directions call for 1/4 cup oil and 2/3 cup kernels to make 4 quarts of popcorn. This works with some brands, but it will make about 6 quarts if the better brands of popcorn are used. That can cause problems in a 4-quart popper. You'll get best results if you use 1/3 as much oil as corn—both measured by volume. In other words, for each measuring cup of popcorn kernels, use 1/3-cup oil.

POPPING TEMPERATURE

Corn will begin to pop when the temperature of the heating surface or the oil reaches 300°F (149°C), although it does not pop *well* until heated above 400°F (204°C). Most electric poppers cycle between 360°F and 480°F (182°C and 249°C). Non-electrics can get hotter. The best popping temperature is about 480°F (249°C).

Generally, a high temperature produces better popcorn, although above 500°F (260°C), the popcorn may scorch. Ironically, even worse scorching may occur in a popper that operates in the lower temperature range because the total popping time is longer. The first pieces that pop may remain in the popper for as much as 5 minutes longer.

POPPING CORN WITHOUT OIL

There are times when it's best to use popcorn this is dry-popped. Making popcorn strings and decorations are two good examples.

Dry popping cannot be done in most electric poppers, but is easy in a non-electric, whether the popper is shaken or stirred. A heavy, deep skillet or a pressure cooker with a non-stick surface will also work. Heat the popper for a minute over medium heat before adding the popcorn. Cover with a screen or lid, making certain the steam can escape. Shake until the popping stops.

GOOD POPPING!

Popping is considered to be good when 1% or less of the kernels fail to pop. There are about 1600 kernels in one cupful. This means that if there are more than 16 kernels left per cup, there is room for improvement in either the popcorn, the oil, the popper or your technique.

TOO DRY OR TOO MOIST?

Moisture content for the greatest popping expansion varies from about 13% to 14.5%. If the moisture is a few percentage points above or below the optimum, the popping volume drops significantly.

Kernels that are too dry pop feebly with a somewhat muffled sound. They may only split partly open, and the unpopped part may be dark and scorched. Kernels that are too moist pop loudly, but the popcorn pieces are small, jagged and tough.

If the proper moisture level is maintained, the age of the kernels makes little difference in popping. A sealed can, glass or plastic jar can keep the moisture constant for years. Cellophane or polyethylene bags hold moisture well if they are not punctured. Moisture loss may occur if the bags are stored for a long period under dry conditions. Popcorn in containers that cannot be tightly re-sealed should be transferred to airtight containers after being opened.

Larry Kusche, a dedicated popcorn enthusiast, presents here an amazing feast of popcorn delectables, popcornology, and little-known facts. Kusche (rhymes with *bush*) invites everyone to munch popcorn made by the methods in this book, while reading another of his bestsellers, *The Bermuda Triangle Mystery—Solved.*

HOW TO CORRECT THE MOISTURE LEVEL

If the pop-ability of your corn is not what it should be, chances are it's too dry. Popcorn rarely gets too moist after it is packaged. Place the too-dry popcorn in an airtight container with 1 teaspoon of water for each 10 ounces liquid measure of kernels. Shake the container several times a day for 2 or 3 days before using. Or, place a damp paper towel in the container and skip the shaking. One teaspoon of water per 10-ounce container, or 1 tablespoon per quart of kernels, will raise the moisture approximately 1-1/2%.

SHOULD UNPOPPED CORN BE REFRIGERATED?

The directions on some brands of popcorn tell you it should be stored in the refrigerator. Others say don't store in the refrigerator because the kernels pop larger and fluffier when they are kept at room temperature. The reason for placing popcorn in the refrigerator is more an attempt to keep the moisture constant than it is to keep the popcorn cool. If you keep it in an airtight container, popcorn doesn't need to be refrigerated. Depending on the contents of the refrigerator, popcorn in a non-airtight package can lose its moisture just as readily in the refrigerator as outside it.

EAR FINESSE AND THE POINT OF DIMINISHING RETURNS

One of the great moments of poppery is when that first kernel explodes. You have your favorite popper filled with the right amount of oil and popcorn kernels. The oil is bubbling and sizzling as you watch and wait expectantly for that sudden bonanza of popped corn.

Then you hear that first tentative little "POP." Popcorn worshippers know that first hesitant, muffled little pop is a promise that every kernel will soon explode in a rising crescendo of glorious popping furor, producing a rising mountain of fluffy popped corn and filling the room with that aroma which brings us back time and again to the popper.

Suddenly the popping tempo slows. The torrent of popping sounds becomes a trickle. Irregular pop-pops, surrounded by silence. An agony of doubt invades the mind. "How many more will pop?" "Will they all pop?" "Have they all popped?" "Is it all over?" "Maybe not, I'll wait a moment longer."

Waiting too long is the problem. You get a few more pops but some of the popped corn in the bottom of the pan scorches and the smell in the room says "Scorched corn!" rather than "Quick, pour on the melted butter!"

The masterful popperperson attends the popper with cunning and ear finesse. The rhythm of popping tells the sophisticated listener when the point of diminishing returns is reached—when the risk of scorching exceeds the benefit of a few more pops.

With perfect timing, the popperperson with ear finesse removes the heat at exactly the right moment. Even the popcorn itself applauds such talent. With the heat off and the popcorn settling down in the pan, it expresses gratitude for not being scorched. It says, "pop, pop!" contentedly

Popcorn With Flavored Butters

Popcorn with butter and salt is the version most of us have grown-up with. But popcorn doesn't have to survive on butter and salt alone. This section of *Popcorn Cookery* will begin to expand your view of popcorn. Try the recipes that appeal to you, then branch out on your own. Experiment with whatever flavors you think will blend well with butter and popcorn. You may even develop a brand-new popcorn recipe!

BUTTER AND ITS SUBSTITUTES

Butter, or a substitutue, does more than add flavor to popcorn. It also acts as a necessary liquid in some recipes, and as an adhesive in others. Without butter, salt will not stick well to popcorn. Butter, margarine, imitation margarine and buttery spreads are generally available in grocery stores. They come in a variety of consistencies, solid, soft, whipped and liquid. They may contain salt, have a low salt content, be unsalted, or be a diet spread. They are made of cream, corn oil, cottonseed oil, safflower oil, soybean oil or vegetable oil and other things. There is some form of butter to fit your taste. Many recipes in this book call for butter, but any of the *substitutes* may be used.

If you use whipped butter, whipped margarine or whipped spread, you may have to use up to 1-1/2 times as much as the recipe calls for to get the right amount of liquid when melted.

Be careful not to leave butter on the heat too long or on too high a heat. Butter burns very easily. It also evaporates. If you leave the heat on after the butter has melted, you may discover you have quite a bit less butter than you started with.

Most recipes in this book call for 1 tablespoon of butter to 1 quart of popped popcorn. This is a moderate amount. If you prefer more or less, adjust the amount accordingly.

Bacon drippings make an interesting substitute for butter. See the section on How to Pop Popcorn, page 15.

HOW TO DRIZZLE BUTTER

The best way to distribute butter evenly over popped popcorn is to put half the popcorn in a large bowl with a rounded bottom. Hold the butter pan in one hand and start rotating the bowl with the other. Allow a very thin stream of butter to trickle from the pan. As you rotate the bowl, slowly and carefully move the butter pan from the edge of the bowl to the center and back again. Do this several times. Watch the butter pan to maintain the thin stream of butter. Occasionally glance at the bowl of popcorn to see how the butter is being distributed. Stop the operation about halfway to stir the popcorn and add salt.

Place the remaining popcorn on top of the buttered popcorn, drizzle with the remaining butter, following the same procedure. Add more salt and mix well.

Another method is to pour butter onto the side of a table knife held over the bowl. This allows the butter to splash over the popcorn and works fine once you get the hang of it.

Or you can drizzle butter from a tablespoon with more control than pouring it directly from the pan.

Apply salt immediately after drizzling the butter. If you butter the popcorn in 2 parts, add salt to the first part before adding and buttering the second part.

If the popcorn is popped some time before it's going to be eaten, do not drizzle the butter until immediately before serving

SIZZLING SAUCES

You can spice up your popcorn butter by adding a few drops of a prepared sauce as the butter melts. Try barbecue sauce, enchilada sauce, hot-pepper sauce, soy sauce or steak sauce. If you add more than a few drops of any of these sauces, decrease the butter an equal amount.

Experiment with a sauce combined with another

ingredient. Chopped chives with butter and hot-pepper sauce is delicious. How about chopped onion with butter and steak sauce, or parsley flakes with butter and Worcestershire sauce? There's an endless variety of possible combinations. Why not create one of your own?

Sautéing tasty ingredients in the popcorn butter is a good way to flavor popcorn. When you saute chopped mushrooms, onions or other delicacies in the butter to be drizzled over the popcorn, add a little extra butter to allow for evaporation and to help spread the chopped pieces of the sautéed ingredient.

The best way to drizzle butter over popcorn is to start with half the popcorn in a bowl. Rotate the bowl while you slowly pour a thin stream of butter over the popcorn.

When you have poured on about half of the melted butter, add the remaining popcorn and repeat the procedure.

MOST OF THE RECIPES CALL FOR 2 QUARTS OF POPPED POPCORN

Although many poppers make up to 4 quarts of popcorn, most of the recipes in this book call for 2 quarts. Four quarts of popped popcorn is quite a lot and you probably would not normally use that much. To make enough for a 3- or 4-quart serving from a 2-quart recipe, simply multiply the ingredients by 1-1/2 or by 2.

Because of the large amount of kernels used when making 3 or 4 quarts, more of the kernels will get swept away from the heat. As a result, there will be more "old maids" left in the bottom of the popper.

Popcorn With Bionic Butter

An extra-strong butter flavor.

3 tablespoons butter
2 qts. popped popcorn

Butter-flavored salt or
    popcorn seasoning to taste

Melt butter over low heat. Drizzle over popcorn. Sprinkle with butter salt or popcorn seasoning. Makes 2 quarts.

Popcorn With Saucy Butter

Use the greens from your garden.

3 tablespoons butter
1 garlic clove
2 teaspoons chives or
    1 teaspoon chopped green onions

1/2 tablespoon chopped parsley
2 qts. popped popcorn
Salt to taste

Melt butter over low heat. Chop garlic into large pieces. Place in butter for 3 to 5 minutes, then remove. Add chives or green onions and parsley. Heat on low heat for 1 minute. Drizzle over popcorn. Add salt to taste. Makes 2 quarts.

Popcorn With Fiesta Butter

A handsome bowlful of western flavors.

2 tablespoons butter
1/3 tablespoon salt
1/3 teaspoon garlic powder
1/3 teaspoon chili powder

1/3 teaspoon parsley flakes
2/3 teaspoon grated Parmesan cheese
2 qts. popped popcorn

Melt butter over low heat. Stir in salt, garlic powder, chili powder, parsley and cheese. Mix thoroughly with the popcorn. Makes 2 quarts.

Popcorn With Onion Butter

Authentic flavor with real onion.

2 tablespoons butter	2 qts. popped popcorn
1 cube chicken bouillon	Salt to taste

Melt butter over low heat. Dissolve bouillon cube in melting butter. Drizzle over popcorn. Add salt to taste. Makes 2 quarts.

Popcorn With Mexicali Butter

Muy bien!

3 tablespoons butter	2 qts. popped popcorn
1/2 tablespoon dry taco-seasoning mix	Salt to taste
1/2 tablespoon dried chopped chives	

Melt butter over low heat. Stir in taco-seasoning mix and chives. Drizzle over popcorn. Add salt to taste. Makes 2 quarts.

Popcorn With Bouillon Butter

Bouillon on popcorn?

2-1/2 tablespoons butter	2 qts. popped popcorn
1 cube chicken bouillon	Salt to taste

Melt butter over low heat. Dissolve bouillon cube in melting butter. Drizzle over popcorn. Add salt to taste. Makes 2 quarts.

Variations:
Use beef, onion, or other flavored bouillon.

Popcorn With Peanut-Butter Butter

Try it. You'll love it!

1 tablespoon peanut butter,
  creamy or chunky
2 tablespoons butter

2 qts. popped popcorn
Salt to taste

Melt peanut butter and butter over low heat until smooth. Pour over popcorn and mix well. Add salt to taste. If desired, increase the amount of peanut butter while decreasing the butter an equal amount.

Variations:
Other nut butters such as almond, cashew, sesame seed or sunflower seed, are available in health food stores.

Popcorn With Mushroom Butter

Mushroom lovers will make quick work of it.

2 tablespoons chopped, bottled or
  fresh mushrooms
3-1/2 tablespoons butter

2 qts. popped popcorn
Salt to taste

Sauté mushrooms in butter over low heat for at least 5 minutes. Do not let the butter burn or reduce to less than 3 tablespoons. Distribute mushroom bits and butter evenly over popcorn. Shake and stir as little as possible, because this will cause more of the mushroom pieces to stick to the sides or settle to the bottom of the bowl. Add salt to taste. Makes 2 quarts.

Variation:
Substitute 1 tablespoon of dehydrated whole mushrooms for bottled or fresh mushrooms.

Popcorn With Cheese-Garlic Butter

Cheesy and buttery. Mmmm.

2 qts. popped popcorn
1/3 cup butter
1/3 cup grated Parmesan or Romano cheese

1 tablespoon minced garlic or
    garlic powder to taste
Salt to taste

Preheat oven to 250°F (121°C). Spread popcorn in a large 4-inch-deep baking pan. Keep warm in the oven. Melt butter and grated cheese over low heat. Stir in minced garlic. Remove popcorn from oven and drizzle with butter mixture, blending until popcorn is thoroughly coated. Add salt to taste. Makes 2 quarts.

Popcorn With Garlic Butter

You won't be able to stop nibbling.

3 tablespoons butter
1 garlic clove, sliced

2 qts. popped popcorn
Salt to taste

Melt butter on low heat. Add garlic and sauté for 3 to 4 minutes. Do not let butter burn or evaporate. Remove garlic. Drizzle butter over popcorn and mix well. Add salt to taste. Makes 2 quarts.

Popcorn With Southwestern Chili Butter

Easterners better not try this one!

2 small dried red or green chilies
2 tablespoons butter
2 qts. popped popcorn

1/4 teaspoon garlic salt
Salt to taste

In covered pan, cook chilies in butter over low heat for 5 minutes. Do not let butter burn or evaporate. Remove chilies. Drizzle butter over popcorn. Season with garlic salt. Add salt to taste. Makes 2 quarts.

Variation:
Dice chilies and pour them over popcorn with the butter.

Popcorn With Chili-Confetti Butter

A lively blend of tangy flavors.

3 qts. popped popcorn
1/4 cup butter
1 teaspoon chili powder

1/2 cup shredded mild-cheddar cheese
3 green onions, including stems, sliced
Salt to taste

Preheat oven to 250°F (121°C). Spread popcorn in a large, 4-inch-deep baking pan. Keep hot in the oven. Heat butter, chili powder, cheese and onions over low heat until both butter and cheese are melted. Do not let mixture burn or evaporate. Remove popcorn from oven. Drizzle with butter-cheese mixture. Add salt to taste. Makes 2 quarts.

Popcorn With Parmesan-Cheese Butter

For cheese lovers—an especially easy blend.

2 qts. popped popcorn
1/2 cup butter

1/2 cup grated Parmesan cheese
Salt to taste

Preheat oven to 250°F (121°C). Spread popcorn in a large, 4-inch-deep baking pan. Keep hot in the oven. Melt butter and grated cheese together over low heat. Mix well. Remove popcorn from oven. Cover with cheese-butter mixture. Stir until every piece is coated. Add salt to taste. Makes 2 quarts.

Variation:
Substitute grated American or Romano cheese for Parmesan cheese.

> **BYE-BYE BUTTER**
> Melt butter carefully over low heat. Butter will burn on high heat and evaporate if left on the heat after it's melted.

Make & Store French Herb Butter

Fifty million Frenchmen can't be wrong!

1/2 cup butter
1 teaspoon lemon juice
1 teaspoon crushed dried parsley flakes
1 teaspoon crushed dried chervil,
   basil or savory

2 teaspoons finely chopped chives
Salt to taste

Allow butter to soften, but not melt, in a small bowl at room temperature. Add lemon juice. Gradually stir in crushed herbs. Spoon into small container. Cover and store in refrigerator. Use within 2 or 3 weeks. Make at least one day before using to give the flavors a chance to blend and mellow. Makes approximately 1/2 cup of butter or enough for 8 quarts of popped popcorn.

Popcorn With Chicken-Flavored Butter

Good munching while watching a TV western.

1/2 teaspoon chicken-flavored broth mix
1/2 teaspoon water
1/4 teaspoon poultry seasoning
1/4 teaspoon celery seed

3 tablespoons butter
2 qts. popped popcorn
Salt to taste

In a small saucepan, mix broth mix, water and poultry seasoning until broth mix is dissolved. Add celery seed and butter. Warm over low heat until butter is melted. Drizzle over popcorn. Add salt to taste. Makes 2 quarts.

Popcorn With Simon & Garfunkel Butter

You'll enjoy this naturally pungent blend.

2 tablespoons butter
1/4 teaspoon crushed dried parsley flakes
Pinch of powdered sage
1/8 teaspoon crushed dried rosemary leaves

1/4 teaspoon crushed dried thyme leaves
1/4 teaspoon lemon juice
2 qts. popped popcorn
Salt to taste

Melt butter over low heat. Stir herbs and lemon juice into the melting butter. Drizzle over popcorn. Add salt to taste. Makes 2 quarts.

Popcorn With French Herb Butter

Garden flavors make a refreshing butter sauce.

2 tablespoons butter
1/4 teaspoon lemon juice
1/4 teaspoon crushed dried parsley flakes
1/4 teaspoon crushed dried chervil,
   basil or savory

1/2 teaspoon finely chopped chives
2 qts. popped popcorn
Salt to taste

Melt butter over low heat. Stir herbs and lemon juice into the melting butter. Drizzle over popcorn. Add salt to taste. Makes 2 quarts.

Crush dried herbs and finely chop fresh herbs.

Measure crushed or chopped herbs and add to unmelted butter. Melt over low heat so the herb flavors permeate the butter as it melts.

Make & Store Simon & Garfunkel Butter

Something from Mrs. Robinson's kitchen.

1/2 cup butter
1 teaspoon lemon juice
1 teaspoon crushed dried parsley flakes
1/4 teaspoon powdered sage

1/2 teaspoon crushed dried rosemary leaves
1 teaspoon crushed dried thyme leaves
Salt to taste

Allow butter to soften, but not melt, in a small bowl at room temperature. Add lemon juice. Gradually stir in herbs. Spoon into small container. Cover and store in refrigerator. Use within 2 or 3 weeks. Make at least one day before using to give the flavors a chance to blend and mellow. Makes approximately 1/2 cup butter or butter for 8 quarts of popped popcorn.

Popcorn With Hamilton's Herb Butter

Lemon juice brings out the herbal flavors.

1/2 teaspoon instant onion flakes
1 teaspoon lemon juice
3 tablespoons butter
1-1/4 teaspoons parsley flakes

Pinch of dill weed
Pinch of thyme
2 qts. popped popcorn
Salt to taste

In a small saucepan, soften onion flakes in lemon juice. Add butter, parsley flakes, dill weed and thyme. Warm over low heat to melt the butter. Drizzle over popcorn. Mix well. Add salt to taste. Makes 2 quarts.

Popcorn With Herb Butter

A classic blend of herb, lemon and butter.

2 tablespoons butter
3/4 to 1-1/2 teaspoons crushed oregano
  or other herb

1/4 teaspoon lemon juice
2 qts. popped popcorn
Salt to taste

Melt butter over low heat. Stir in crushed herb and lemon juice. Drizzle butter over popcorn. Add salt to taste. Makes 2 quarts.

Make & Store Herb Butter

Choose your own herb for a personal touch.

1/2 cup butter
1 teaspoon lemon juice

1 to 2 tablespoons crushed oregano
    or other herb

Allow butter to soften, but not melt, in a small bowl at room temperature. Add lemon juice. Gradually stir in crushed herbs. Spoon into small container. Cover and store in refrigerator. Use within 2 or 3 weeks. Make at least one day before using to give the flavors a chance to blend and mellow. Makes approximately 1/2 cup of butter or enough for 8 quarts of popped popcorn.

Popcorn With Jerky Butter

Here's a way to add protein to your popcorn.

2 (1-1/8-oz.) pkgs. dried jerky, chopped
2 tablespoons butter

2 qts. popped popcorn
Salt to taste

Cook jerky in melting butter over low heat for several minutes, Do not let butter burn or evaporate. Pour over popcorn. Mix well. Add salt to taste. Serve immediately. Makes 2 quarts.

Variations:
Substitute salami, pepperoni or Polish sausage for jerky.

Popcorn With Chili-Cheese Sauce

Just a little picante.

3 tablespoons butter
1/3 tablespoon chili powder
1/3 cup grated cheddar cheese

2 qts. popped popcorn
Salt to taste

In a small saucepan, melt butter over low heat. Combine chili powder and cheese together. Add to melted butter and mix well. Return to low heat until cheese is partially melted. Drizzle over popcorn. Add salt to taste. Makes 2 quarts.

The History of Popcorn

No one knows who deserves the credit for "discovering" popcorn, but popcorn lovers are grateful for the discovery. Its use goes back far beyond the earliest writings. It was probably discovered accidentally when one of our ancient ancestors held an ear of corn over a fire, heard it make a funny noise and saw a "little white flower" mysteriously grow on its side. The sense of wonder that discovery must have inspired, and the good taste of the "white flower" have been a part of popcorn since the beginning.

There is evidence that popcorn may have been the first type of corn raised for human consumption. Ancient clay and metal poppers have been found in many parts of Mexico, South America and the southwestern United States. Ears of popcorn 5600 years old were found by archeologists in the Bat Cave in New Mexico in 1948.

Corn was not known in Europe until its introduction by Christopher Columbus after his return from the West Indies. He found the natives of the New World not only eating popcorn, but wearing it in decorations like corsages.

The early explorers of North and South America saw popcorn used in many ways by the natives. In 1519, Cortez found Aztecs using popcorn as an important food, as a decoration on ceremonial headdresses, and as ornaments for the statues of their gods. They honored their god of the fisherman by scattering popcorn before him. Young maidens placed garlands of popped popcorn over their heads to honor the god of war. Some Indian tribes tossed kernels into the fire to predict their fortunes, predicting the future from how many kernels popped and in which direction they flew. Even today, it is part of the life style in Guatemala, occupying a quasi-religious position in the social and political lives of the people.

We think popcorn was introduced to the English colonists at the first Thanksgiving feast at Plymouth, Massachusetts. According to the legend, Quadequina, the brother of a local chief, brought a deerskin bag full of popped popcorn to the dinner as a gift. Later, popcorn came to be a sign of peace. It was often shared as a token of goodwill when the Indians and colonists met for negotiations.

For two centuries popcorn was almost exclusively home grown and home popped. Just about every farmer grew some popcorn for his own use. Sometimes farmers sold a little at the local marketplace, but nobody went into the business on a large scale. Historians have found little mention of popcorn in early American writings, and no commercial use until the 1880's.

POPULARIZING POPCORN

In 1885 Charles Cretors of Chicago invented the first popping machine, which was powered by steam. He also developed the wet popper— popping the corn in oil. Until then it had always been dry-popped. Traveling salesmen began taking orders for Cretors' poppers and the popcorn business began to grow.

The next step was to place the popping machines on wheels so they could be moved about. Small popcorn wagons were pulled by ponies; large popcorn wagons were horse-drawn or mounted on truck frames. Popcorn wagons quickly became familiar sights at street corners, county fairs, circuses, political rallies, band concerts and outdoor gatherings of all kinds. Their familiar aroma and the commotion they caused when the popcorn popped, made them welcome everywhere.

Charles Cretors introduced salesmanship to the business. He believed that the best advertising was the popping of the popcorn itself. If the machine was full, Cretors would give the popcorn away, not only to make room to pop more, but to attract attention and cause other customers to head in his direction. Once a line formed it usually grew longer.

Many people still grew small patches of popcorn in their home gardens, and those who could not grow it began buying it. In 1897, the Sears, Roebuck catalog listed popcorn—25 pounds, on

Improved No. 2 Wagon

An obvious improvement on the Cretors Improved Number 2 Wagon is the canopy.

This popcorn machine installed on a Stanley Steamer will interest both popcorn fans and old-car buffs.

This handsome 1922 Ford Model TT is equipped with a Cretors Popcorn Wagon body. Photo courtesy of The Craven Foundation, 760 Lawrence Ave. W., Toronto, Ontario, Canada.

the cob, in a paper sack, for $1.00. Some stores began carrying popcorn on the cob in open barrels, and by the start of the new century, popcorn was well known in many parts of the U.S. In 1914, Cloid Smith of Iowa began packing his Jolly Time® popcorn in 1-pound cardboard containers for local grocery stores.

In 1952, Orville Redenbacher, Charles Bowman and Carl Hartman began developing hybrid popcorn for improved popping quality. This led to Orville Redenbacher Gourmet® Popping Corn which is on the market today.

POPCORN AT THE MOVIES

Some of the things we take for granted today only came about after years of determined effort. As movies became popular, attempts were made to sell popcorn in theaters, but few establishments would allow it. Popcorn was too messy, and many of the customers complained that it smelled and was too noisy. But vendors who set their popcorn wagons outside the theaters found an eager public.

During the depression of the 1930's, theater owners began breaking down and purchasing poppers for their lobbies. In many cases popcorn wagons were sitting just outside the theaters anyway, and confectionary shops were often built next door to theaters. If a manager banned these outside goodies from his theater, the customers quickly took their business to another theater. Grudgingly, the theater owners decided they might just as well get the profit that was going to the venders outside.

The poppers were placed, and today are still placed, where the customers have to pass them to get to their seats. Rarely, if ever, is a concession stand placed off to the side, out of the way of traffic. Before long, candy, sodas and ice cream were also being sold in the lobbies.

Most of the next-door confectionaries went out of business soon after a concession stand opened in a theater. The popcorn vendors in the street fared better. In many cases they had been "plants"—part of a team working to convince the theaters to

sell popcorn. Charles T. Manley of Kansas City used this method and was very successful in engineering the breakthrough into theaters. It was not long before a common saying was, "Find a good popcorn location and build a theater around it."

By 1947, 85% of the nation's theaters sold popcorn and other treats. The surprising part is that the remaining 15% did not. Popcorn was bringing millions of "extra" dollars to the theaters and enjoyment to millions of people. In many cases the concession stands brought in almost as much income as admissions did.

On the West Coast they went so far as to build large, ornate concession counters surrounded with neon-light displays. These stands led to another innovation in theaters, the intermission. The lights would come on for 10 to 15 minutes to allow customers plenty of time to get to the lobby and back. In some theaters, girls dressed in evening gowns walked up and down the aisles informing the audience about the delicious treats available. Later, "promos" showing all the goodies that could be found in the lobby were run on the screen just before the lights came on.

THE GREAT POPCORN SLUMP

Movie theaters changed popcorn from small to big business. In 1900 there were about 20,000 acres devoted to growing popcorn in the U.S. In 1920 there were 60,000. By 1948 this figure had grown to 300,000 acres.

Then, disaster! Movie attendance began falling drastically about 1949. And popcorn consumption fell at the same rate. People were staying home in droves to stare at a tiny, flashing black-and-white box called television.

Theaters began folding and the market was flooded with used commercial poppers and warmers. 1950 was especially hard on the popcorn business and it was apparent that new markets were needed.

The directors of the Popcorn Institute, an association of popcorn processors, thought that the people who were used to eating popcorn at the

The march of progress brought us this Cretors machine installed on an early truck chassis.

movies might be persuaded that it was just as good at home. Many people already popped popcorn at home, but most people still associated popcorn only with movies. The problem was not how to introduce popping at home. The problem was how to revive a custom that had declined.

The Institute persuaded the Coca-Cola Company that Coke® was always best when drunk with something else. Why not make that something else popcorn? Popcorn, in turn, makes a person thirsty. What better way is there to quench thirst than with a Coke®?

The Morton Salt Company also advertised popcorn with the slogan, "Popcorn worth its salt is worth Morton's." Some breweries and salad-oil companies also advertised with popcorn complimenting their products, and people began popping at home.

By late 1951 the sale of unpopped corn was climbing. The increase was caused by the same thing that had caused the initial slump—television. A survey of TV owners in Chicago found that 4% ate popcorn every night, 10% had it 5 or 6 nights a week, and 63% had it 1 to 4 nights. That leaves 23% who claimed not to eat it at all. But tele-

vision owners were still in the minority, and by 1952 only about 25% of the popcorn being produced was popped in the home. Still, all previous records were broken that year when more than $250,000,000 worth of popcorn was sold. The sale of electric home poppers also began to increase, and it appeared that the Great Popcorn Slump may have ended by 1952.

POPCORN MAKES GOOD (EATING)

Popcorn was rapidly becoming as popular at home as it once was at the movies. Despite the drop in theater attendance, overall popcorn consumption reached new highs each year. In 1952 about 65% of the sales had been in theaters. Five years later, more than half the popcorn produced was popped at home. There were 40,000,000 television sets in the country, turned on for an average of 6 hours each day. It was like having your own movie theater—and concession stand—at home.

Today, 2/3 of all the popcorn produced in the world is consumed in the American home, much of it in the evening or on weekends in front of the television.

This sieve was used by the Iroquois Indians to separate unpopped kernels from popped corn.

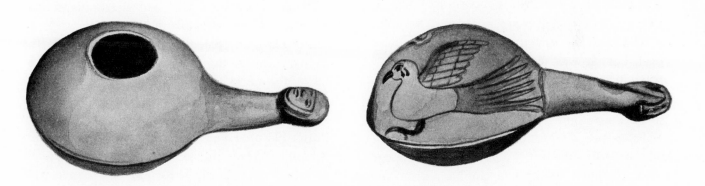

Ancient pottery poppers similar to this one from Peru were widely used in North and South America before Columbus.

Salty Snacks

POPCORN ON THE ROAD

If you're traveling and making nightly stops at motels or hotels, take along your electric popper and a supply of popcorn. You'll have a healthy snack without a long, fatiguing search for a food store. Butter, salt and popcorn packed in popping oil come in handy here. Take along a few containers of special flavorings, such as Parmesan Cheese, garlic powder or imitation bacon bits. They make the snack so much better.

The next time you go to a drive-in movie, don't forget your own fresh popcorn. Before you leave the house, pop the popcorn and drizzle it with your favorite flavored butter. Pour it into a double-thick grocery bag and you have the evening's supply of popcorn made the way you like it best.

For a delicious on-the-road or after-school snack, hand out containers of yogurt or fresh fruit and small bags of popped popcorn.

Wouldn't you like some popcorn right now?

SALT AND ITS SUBSTITUTES

People on low-salt diets need not be deprived of the good taste of buttery, salted popcorn. Imitation salt-free butter, made with safflower, soybean or other oils, is available. You can also buy salt substitutes.

Try popcorn with no butter and just a touch of salt or salt substitute. Salt enhances popcorn's naturally nutty flavor and emphasizes the flavor of the popping oil.

There are a variety of salts on the market:

Popcorn Salt—A very fine-grained salt that covers the popcorn pieces more uniformly than other salts. It is also less likely to settle to the bottom of the bowl. Most grocery stores carry popcorn salt.

Table Salt—Usually much coarser than popcorn salt and does not coat the popcorn pieces as evenly.

Half Salt—A mixture of table salt (sodium chloride) and potassium chloride, for people who wish to reduce their sodium intake.

Dietetic Salt Substitute—For people who have been advised to exclude sodium from their diets. The flavor differs only slightly from table salt.

Sea Salt—Available in health food stores. It is said to be lower in sodium and higher in minerals and other nutrients than other salts. Sea salt has the same flavor as table salt.

Half salt, dietetic salt and sea salt come only in a coarse grain, but you can turn them into a fine grain by placing several tablespoonfuls in a blender for a few minutes. Be certain the lid is tightly sealed or your house and yard will be covered with salt dust. Leave the lid on for a least 5 minutes after turning the blender off to let the dust settle.

Table salt is the least expensive of all the salts. But the cost of the most expensive salt is small and does not need to be a factor in shopping for popcorn-recipe ingredients.

SEASONED SALTS

Prepared seasoned salts add instant flavor and interest to a bowl of popcorn.

Butter-Flavored Salt—Eliminates the need for melted butter, although there is a taste difference. Butter-flavored salt sticks to dry popcorn. You can buy yellow or white butter-flavored salt. It may be a mixture of coarse and fine grains.

Butter-Flavored Popcorn Salt or **Buttery Popcorn Seasoning**—These are salt-based products made especially for popcorn. They may be flavored with butter-related products or with artificial flavorings. Some directions recommend using these products as you would salt. Others suggest that they be added to the popping oil before the popping starts, or to the butter before pouring it over the popcorn. At least one popcorn company includes a package of buttery seasoning in each package of popcorn.

Some other seasoned salts are: barbecue salt, chili salt, garlic salt, hamburger-seasoning salt, kelp salt, lemon-pepper salt and sesame salt. Most of

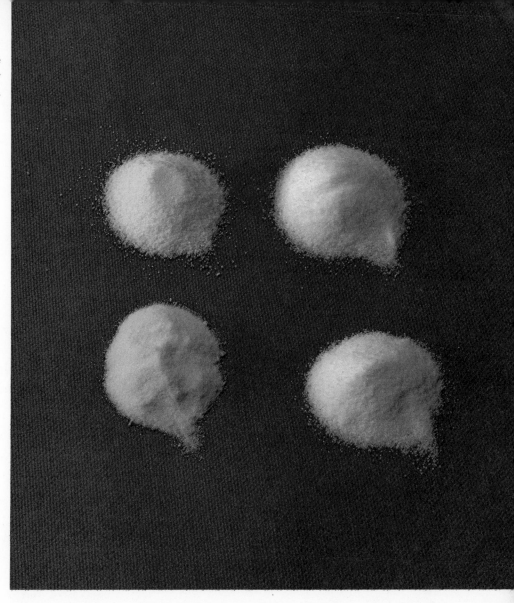

Salts: Clockwise from top right, these are—table salt, popcorn salt, butter flavored popcorn salt, butter salt.

these are coarse grained like table salt, but can be finely ground in a blender, if you prefer. You may wish to use flavored salt mixed with plain salt to avoid an overwhelming flavor of such potent ingredients as garlic or onions.

HOMEMADE SEASONED SALTS

Make flavored salts right in your own kitchen. Ground spices and crushed herbs can be sprinkled directly on buttered popcorn, but they tend to stick together in small clumps. They will spread more evenly if you first mix them with salt. For most homemade salts, try 2 parts spice or crushed herb with 3 parts salt. Some suggestions are: cumin, mace, oregano, poultry seasoning, saffron, tarragon and turmeric.

Some spices and herbs are stronger than others. Take this into consideration when preparing homemade salts. For example: Use 1 part cream of tartar to 2 parts salt. Use 1 part garlic powder to 3 parts salt. Use 1 part ginger to 1 part salt. Use 1 part mustard powder to 1 part salt.

If you find a flavor you especially like, make a large batch of it. Or you can make a variety of seasoned salts and store them in small salt shakers.

SALTY RECIPES WITH OTHER INGREDIENTS

Because salty recipes are not sticky, additional ingredients such as cheese or grated meat may fall to the bottom of the bowl and not stay mixed in with the popcorn. If that happens, spread the popcorn on a pan and cover it with the additional ingredients. Then lift the popcorn off the pan with a spatula and place it in layers in individual serving bowls. If cheese is one of the ingredients, place the mixture in the oven just long enough for the cheese to start melting. When you remove the cheese-popcorn mixture from the pan with a spatula, take care not to let it break apart.

SEED AND HERB GARNISHES

Herbs and seeds can be used to flavor popcorn. Some, such as parsley flakes, can be crushed by hand. Others, such as dill seed, can be chopped in the blender, although this isn't absolutely necessary. Soft, mild-flavored seeds, such as sesame and caraway, need not be chopped.

About 1 teaspoon of garnish, measured before crushing, is an average amount per quart of popped popcorn. Butter popcorn as usual, then sprinkle the crushed garnish over it. Salt to taste. DO NOT STIR. Stirring will cause some of the garnish to settle to the bottom of the bowl. If necessary, sprinkle with garnish and salt again when the bowl is half empty.

If you prefer, sauté half of the garnish in 2 tablespoons of butter and drizzle it over the popcorn. Sprinkle the other half over the popcorn after drizzling with the garnished butter. Some flavorful garnishes are: basil leaves, cardamom seeds, chervil, chopped chives, fennel, and oregano.

HERB TEA GARNISHES

Delicious herb teas are available. Most of them can be used to flavor popcorn. Crush the leaves of the herb tea very fine. You may have to use a blender. Sprinkle the crushed herb-tea leaves directly over the buttered popcorn. Or, sauté them in butter for several minutes before pouring the butter over the popcorn. Use 1/2 to 1 teaspoon of herb-tea leaves, measured before crushing, to 1 quart of popped popcorn. Double this amount if you use fresh herbs. Salt to taste.

To make herb-tea salt, place 2 or more parts herb-tea leaves, depending on the strength of the herb, and 1 part salt in a blender for a few minutes. The mixture can be stored in a small covered container for long periods of time or in a salt shaker for immediate use.

POWDERED-SEASONING MIXES

A variety of powdered seasoning mixes for salads and entrees is on the market. Before using these mixes to flavor your popcorn, check the ingredient list on the packet. If you are making salty popcorn, do not use a mix containing sugar or other sweeteners.

There are 3 ways of adding a powdered mix to popcorn:

1. Sprinkle the powdered mix over buttered, popped popcorn.

2. Stir half the powdered mix into melted butter. Drizzle the seasoned butter over the popcorn, then sprinkle the remaining powdered mix over the buttered and seasoned popcorn.

3. Stir all the powdered mix slowly into melted butter, making sure that the butter remains pourable. If the butter begins to get thick, stop stirring in the powdered mix before the butter becomes too stiff and pour it on the popcorn.

Some of the powdered mixes will have a more pervasive flavor when applied with method 2 or 3. Do not add powdered mixes to butter in a butter dispenser.

Here are some suggestions for powdered-seasoning mixes: chicken-sauce mix, chili-sauce mix, enchilada-sauce mix, hamburger seasoning, hollandaise-sauce mix, pork seasoning, sour-cream mix, spaghetti-sauce mix, sweet-and-sour sauce mix, and teriyaki-sauce mix.

POWDERED DIP MIXES

These mixes make tasty additions to popcorn. You can either stir the powdered dip mix into butter or sprinkle the mix over the popcorn after drizzling butter over popcorn. Use 1-1/2 to 2 teaspoons of powdered dip-mix to 2 tablespoons of butter.

Some available mixes are: avacado, bleu cheese, chili, clam, cucumber, garlic, jalapeño and sour cream.

POWDERED SOUP MIXES

Instant soup mixes can also flavor your popcorn very quickly. Be sure the mix does not contain

than coarsely grated cheese. Some cheeses good for mixing with popcorn are: Gouda, Monterey Jack, mozzarella and Swiss cheese. Pre-grated cheeses such as Parmesan, Romano and American cheese, stick to the popcorn better than the home-grated ones.

Kraft's powdered Cheddar cheese is the best I've found for getting cheese onto popcorn. Because it is so finely powdered, it is easy to coat every kernel to ensure cheese flavor in every bite. Unfortunately, you have to buy it in 20-pound cartons at restaurant food suppliers, but it's worth the trouble to get it.

MISCELLANEOUS FLAVORINGS

Your cupboard shelves contain a number of staple items to add fun and new tastes to popcorn. Start with 2 quarts of popped popcorn for each flavor variation.

Wheat Germ—Melt 2-1/2 tablespoons of butter and drizzle over the popcorn. Sprinkle with 1 to 2 tablespoons of wheat germ. Add salt to taste.

Powdered Milk—Melt 2 tablespoons of butter. Stir in 2 tablespoons of powdered milk and drizzle it over the popcorn. Add salt or sugar to taste.

Unsweetened Drink-Mix Flavors—Melt 2 tablespoons of butter and stir in 1 teaspoon of unsweetened-drink-mix flavor, such as lemon, lime or orange. Drizzle it over the popcorn. Add salt to taste.

Instant-Tea Powder—Melt 2 tablespoons of butter. Drizzle it over the popcorn and sprinkle with 4 teaspoons of instant-tea powder. Add salt to taste.

Prepared Mustard—Melt 2 tablespoons of butter. Slowly stir in 1 tablespoon of prepared mustard. Drizzle butter-mustard mixture over the popcorn and mix well. Add salt to taste. Substitute 1 to 2 teaspoons of mustard powder, if you prefer.

Alfalfa Sprouts—Melt 2 tablespoons of butter and drizzle it over the popcorn. Chop 1 cup of alfalfa sprouts. Sprinkle them over the popcorn and add salt to taste. You can use 3/4 cup of bean sprouts, if you prefer.

Bacon—Melt 2 tablespoons of butter. Drizzle it over the popcorn. Crumble 2 very crisply fried and drained slices of bacon and sprinkle over the popcorn. If you prefer, use 1 tablespoon of imitation-bacon bits.

sugar or other sweetening agents. Use 1 to 2 tablespoons of powdered soup to 2-1/2 tablespoons of butter. Chop or remove any large pieces from the soup mix before adding to the melted butter, or sprinkling it over buttered popcorn.

Some popular flavors are: bean, green pea, mushroom, onion and potato.

SALAD DRESSINGS

You can get a variety of flavors for your popcorn with salad dressings, either in liquid form or dry mix. Mixes containing sugar or other sweetening agents will confuse your taste buds. Check the ingredients before using. Use 1-1/2 to 2 teaspoons salad dressing, either prepared or dry mix, to 2-1/2 tablespoons of butter. Stir the salad dressing or dry mix into the melted butter and drizzle over the popcorn. If you are using a dry mix, you can either add it to the melted butter or sprinkle it over the buttered popcorn.

CHEESE AND POPCORN

Many types of cheese can be used to add flavor to popcorn. The easiest method is to grate them. To avoid having some of the grated cheese settle to the bottom of the bowl, place the mixture in a 300°F (149°C) oven in a heat-proof bowl for 3 to 5 minutes or until the cheese just melts. Finely grated cheese is less likely to settle to the bottom

Party Mix

A new ingredient for a traditional favorite.

1/4 cup butter or margarine
1/2 teaspoon garlic salt
1/2 teaspoon onion salt
1/4 teaspoon celery salt
1-1/2 tablespoons Worcestershire sauce

1/8 teaspoon Tabasco® sauce
2 qts. popped popcorn
1 cup pretzel sticks
1-1/2 cups salted mixed nuts

Preheat oven to 275°F (135°C). Melt the butter over low heat. Add garlic salt, onion salt, celery salt, Worcestershire sauce and Tabasco® sauce. Mix thoroughly. Spread the popcorn, pretzel sticks and nuts in a large, shallow baking pan. Drizzle with the butter mixture and toss to mix. Bake in the oven for 1 hour, stirring 4 or 5 times. Cool. Store in a tightly covered container. Makes 2 quarts.

Popcorn No. 5

An exclusive blend for particular people.

2 tablespoons butter
3 to 5 drops hot-pepper sauce
2 qts. popped popcorn
2/3 tablespoon chili powder
1 teaspoon ground cumin
1/3 teaspoon ground coriander

1/4 teaspoon celery salt
1/8 teaspoon onion salt
1/8 teaspoon cayenne pepper
1/8 teaspoon garlic powder
1 cup grated cheddar cheese

Preheat oven to 250°F (121°C). Melt butter over low heat. Stir in hot-pepper sauce. Mix together. Spread popcorn in a large, shallow baking pan. Drizzle with the melted-butter mixture. Mix together all other ingredients except cheese. Sprinkle over buttered popcorn, then sprinkle with grated cheese. Heat in the oven until cheese just begins to melt. Makes 2 quarts.

Buttered & Salted Popcorn

The overwhelmingly favorite way to eat popcorn.

2 tablespoons butter

2 qts. popped popcorn

Salt to taste

Melt butter slowly over low heat. Drizzle over popcorn, stirring to coat the pieces evenly. Add salt to taste. Makes 2 quarts.

Curry Popcorn

Add more cayenne if you like it hotter.

2 tablespoons butter

1 teaspoon curry powder

3/4 teaspoon turmeric

3/4 teaspoon ginger

Pinch of cayenne pepper

2 qts. popped popcorn

Salt to taste

Melt butter over low heat. Drizzle over popcorn. Mix spices together and sprinkle over buttered popcorn. Add salt to taste. Makes 2 quarts.

Chicken-Little Popcorn

An ingenious blend of savory salts and herbs.

3 tablespoons butter

2 qts. popped popcorn

2 individual envelopes instant
  chicken-flavored broth mix

1 teaspoon instant minced onion

1 teaspoon marjoam

1 teaspoon parsley flakes

1/2 teaspoon sage

1/2 teaspoon celery seed

Salt to taste

Melt butter over low heat. Drizzle butter over popcorn. Combine chicken-flavored broth mix, onion, marjoram, parsley, sage and celery seed. Sprinkle over buttered popcorn and toss well. Add salt to taste. Makes 2 quarts.

Shrimp Popcorn

Made to order for seafood lovers.

3 tablespoons butter
3 tablespoons shredded shrimp,
   divided in half

2 qts. popped popcorn
Salt to taste

Melt butter over low heat, adding half the shredded shrimp as butter melts. Spread shrimp thinly, allowing the flavor to permeate the butter for 3 to 5 minutes. Do not let the butter burn or evaporate. Drizzle the butter-shrimp mixture over the popcorn. Mix well. Sprinkle the remaining shrimp over all. Add salt to taste. Makes 2 quarts.

Variation:
Whole shrimp in a side dish goes well with buttered popcorn and lemonade or beer.

Cheese Dog

Larry's favorite lunch. Try it with ice-cold beer or lemonade.

2 qts. butter popped popcorn
2 weiners, finely chopped
Prepared mustard to taste

5 tablespoons finely grated cheese
Salt to taste

Preheat oven to 350°F (177°C). Spread buttered popcorn in a large, shallow baking pan. Sprinkle with chopped weiners. Place in the oven for about 5 minutes. Remove from oven and dab or spread mustard on popcorn with a knife or squeeze-bottle. Sprinkle with cheese. Heat in the oven until cheese just melts. Pieces will break apart easily. Remove with a spatula, placing them flat in individual bowls. Add salt to taste. Makes 2 quarts.

Variation:
Substitute 3 tablespoons of finely grated ham for weiners. Add a teaspoon of grated onion or drained relish with the cheese.

Cheddar Toss 'N Heat

Good with sweet cider or milk.

1/3 cup butter or margarine, melted
4 qts. popped popcorn
1/2 teaspoon garlic salt

1/2 teaspoon onion salt
2 cups shredded sharp-cheddar cheese

Preheat oven to 325°F (163°C). Melt butter over low heat. Pour the popcorn into a large 4-inch-deep baking pan. Add butter, garlic salt, onion salt and cheese, a small amount of each at a time, and toss. Heat in the oven for 5 to 10 minutes to melt the cheese, stirring gently once or twice. Makes 4 quarts.

Shake-'N-Bake® Popcorn

An unusual flavor treat.

4 tablespoons butter
2 qts. popped popcorn

6 tablespoons Shake-'n-Bake®
    for chicken or pork
Salt to taste

Preheat oven to 250°F (121°C). Melt butter over low heat. Pour over popcorn. Spread buttered popcorn in large, shallow baking pan. Sprinkle with Shake-'n-Bake®. Place in oven for 10 minutes. Add salt to taste. Makes 2 quarts.

Variation:
Add a small amount of grated cheese.

Shoestring Mix

Good and salty. Have a cold drink in reach.

4 tablespoons butter
1-1/2 qts. popped popcorn
4 cups pretzel rings

1 (4-oz.) can shoestring potatoes
1 tablespoon onion-soup mix

Preheat oven to 325°F (163°C). Melt butter over low heat. Combine popcorn, pretzel rings and shoestring potatoes in a 13" x 9" baking pan. Add onion-soup mix to butter and stir. Drizzle over popcorn mixture, stirring to coat evenly. Heat in oven for 10 minutes, stirring once. Makes approximately 2-1/2 quarts.

Snack Mixup

Enjoy this spicy snack!

1/3 cup butter
2 qts. popped popcorn
5 to 6 cups slim pretzel sticks
3 to 4 cups cheese curls

2/3 teaspoon Worcestershire sauce
2/3 teaspoon garlic salt
2/3 teaspoon seasoned salt

Preheat oven to 250°F (121°C). Melt butter over low heat. In a large, 4-inch-deep pan, lightly toss together popcorn, pretzel sticks and cheese curls. Combine melted butter and Worcestershire sauce. Drizzle over popcorn, mixing well. Sprinkle with salts. Heat in oven, stirring occasionally, until heated through, about 15 minutes. Makes about 3 quarts.

Tangy Salt

Not only an herbal salt—it's a conversation piece, too.

6 tablespoons salt
2 teaspoons paprika
1 teaspoon dry mustard
1/2 teaspoon garlic salt
1/2 teaspoon celery salt

1/2 teaspoon thyme
1/2 teaspoon marjoram
1/2 teaspoon curry powder
1/2 teaspoon dill weed

Mix all ingredients together in blender. Store in a covered jar or salt shaker. Use on buttered popcorn as desired. Makes 1/2 cup.

Popcorn Medley

A tantalizing blend of textures and spices.

6 tablespoons butter
1 tablespoon Worcestershire sauce
1 teaspoon seasoned salt
1/2 teaspoon garlic powder
1 qt. popped popcorn

1 (3-oz.) can chow-mein noodles
1-1/2 cups bite-size shredded wheat
1 cup pecan halves
1 teaspoon basil

Preheat oven to 250°F (121°C). Melt butter in a large skillet over low heat. Add Worcestershire sauce, seasoned salt and garlic powder. Stir together popcorn, noodles, shredded wheat and pecans. Drizzle butter mixture over all. Toss gently until well-coated. Sprinkle with basil. Spread in a large, shallow baking pan. Heat in oven for 45 minutes, stirring occasionally. Cool. Makes 2 quarts.

Anchovy Popcorn

Just what anchovy lovers have been waiting for.

1/2 can flat anchovies
4 tablespoons butter
1/2 teaspoon garlic powder
1/2 teaspoon lemon-pepper seasoning
3 qts. popped popcorn

2 cups small crisp croutons or
  fried onion rings
2 tablespoons grated Romano cheese
Salt to taste

Drain the anchovy oil into a small saucepan. Chop anchovies very fine. Add to oil in saucepan. Add butter, garlic powder and lemon-pepper seasoning. Heat over low heat to melt butter. Combine popcorn and croutons or onion rings. Drizzle anchovy-butter mixture slowly over popcorn, tossing to mix. Sprinkle with cheese and toss again. Add salt to taste. Makes 3-1/2 quarts.

SOME STATISTICS

The annual production of popcorn has been increasing at an astonishing rate during recent years. In 1966 about 313,000,000 pounds were sold. Sales increased about 10,000,000 pounds a year until, in 1974, they were about 400,000,000 pounds. By 1976, production had zoomed to over 600,000,000 pounds.

After subtracting the amount sent abroad or saved for planting, the average consumption of popcorn per person in the United States is about 2-1/2 pounds, or almost 40 quarts of popped corn, a year. That's a lot of good crunching!

Sweet Snacks

HAVE A POPCORN PARTY!

Send out invitations to a popcorn party. Arrange a variety of butters and sweet powdered mixes buffet-style on a long table. Place heaping bowls of popcorn at each end of the table and give your guests small individual bowls to fill. Then let them drizzle and sprinkle whatever they choose over their own popcorn. Fill several large pitchers with a variety of beverages. Your Popcorn Party will be a topic of conversation for a long time.

Popcorn can be very satisfying for a sweet-tooth craving. Many sweetened flavorings now available can turn plain popcorn into a delightful sugary treat. For various methods of adding flavored-powder mixes to popcorn, see the section on Powdered-Seasoning Mixes on page 38.

Here are some flavoring suggestions for your Popcorn Party or for your own sweet snacks:

Start with 2 quarts of popped popcorn. If buttered popcorn is called for, melt 2 tablespoons of butter and drizzle it over the popcorn.

Sugar—First try plain sugar, white or brown. Dissolve in 1 to 2 tablespoons of melting butter. Drizzle over popcorn.

Orange Breakfast-Drink Powder—Sprinkle 3 tablespoons of orange breakfast-drink powder over buttered popcorn.

Powdered Milk—Stir 2 tablespoons of powdered milk into 2 tablespoons of melting butter. Drizzle over popcorn and sprinkle with sugar to taste.

Powdered Non-Dairy Creamer—Mix 1-1/2 tablespoons of powdered non-dairy creamer and 1 tablespoon of sugar together. Sprinkle over buttered popcorn.

Powdered Cocoa Mix—Combine 2 tablespoons of powdered, sweetened cocoa mix with 1 tablespoon of sugar. Sprinkle over buttered popcorn.

Instant Coffee Powder—Mix 2 teaspoons of instant coffee powder with 2 tablespoons of sugar. Sprinkle over buttered popcorn. If you prefer an international coffee flavor, use 1 teaspoon of international coffee powder instead.

Pure or Imitation Liquid Extracts—Melt 2 tablespoons of butter. Stir in 1 to 2 teaspoons of liquid extract. Drizzle over the popcorn and sprinkle with sugar to taste. Some interesting flavors to try are almond, banana, brandy, coconut, lemon, pineapple, rum, strawberry or vanilla.

Powdered Cocktail Mixes—You can make popcorn with a tangy sweet-sour taste by dissolving 1 or more tablespoons of a powdered cocktail mix in 2 tablespoons of butter. Drizzle over popcorn, mix well and add sugar to taste. Some powdered cocktail mixes are Daiquiri, Gimlet, Piña Colada, Screwdriver, Tequila Sunrise and Whiskey Sour. In case you're wondering, these powdered mixes contain no alcohol.

Colored Cake Decorations—To add color to plain sugared popcorn or, for that matter, to any sweet popcorn, sprinkle it with colored cake decorations. Use any color or color combinations. This adds a nice touch to a Popcorn Party.

NO-STICK
To reduce stickiness in recipes with sugar, place the sugar-coated popcorn in a 300°F (149°C) oven for 3 to 5 minutes.

Strawberry-Malt Popcorn

Pink and pleasing.

4 tablespoons butter
2 qts. popped popcorn
4 tablespoons malt powder

1/2 cup powdered,
    sweetened strawberry-drink mix

Melt butter over low heat. Drizzle over popcorn and mix. Combine malt powder and strawberry-drink mix. Sprinkle over popcorn and toss well to coat evenly. Makes 2 quarts.

Variation:
Substitute another flavored-drink mix for strawberry.

Peanut Butter & Jelly Popcorn

Uses a lot less peanut butter and jelly than sandwiches!

1 tablespoon butter
1 tablespoon peanut butter

1 tablespoon jelly
2 qts. popped popcorn

Melt butter, peanut butter and jelly together over low heat. Drizzle over the popcorn. Mix well to coat all pieces thoroughly. Makes 2 quarts.

Chocolate-Mint Popcorn

A sweet accompaniment with after-dinner coffee.

2 tablespoons butter
6 (1-inch) chocolate-covered mints

2 qts. popped popcorn

Melt butter and mints together over low heat. Pour over popcorn and mix to thoroughly coat all the pieces. Makes 2 quarts.

Russian-Tea Popcorn

The mix, without the popcorn, makes a delicious hot or iced tea.

1/2 cup sugar
1/2 cup powdered orange breakfast-drink mix
1/6 cup lemon-flavored instant tea

1/4 teaspoon cinnamon
1/8 teaspoon ground cloves
2 qts. buttered popped popcorn

Combine all ingredients except popcorn. Mix well. Sprinkle several tablespoons of spice mixture over the buttered popcorn. Store the remainder in a covered container, or use to make tea. Makes 2 quarts of popcorn with approximately 3/4 cup spice mixture left over.

Sugar-Coated Popcorn

To make this, use a popper with a stirring rod.

3 tablespoons butter-flavored
   popping oil

3/8 cup unpopped corn
1/2 cup sugar

Place the oil in the popper over medium-high heat. After the oil becomes hot add the unpopped corn and sugar. Crank continuously until the corn is popped, then empty immediately onto a large, flat pan. With a spoon, separate into individual pieces as the popcorn cools. Do not touch by hand for several minutes as the sugar coating gets very hot. Any clumps of popcorn that remain together will probably come apart when they are handled. Makes 3 quarts.

Variation:
Add 2 rounded teaspoons of chocolate powder or malt powder with the sugar and pop as directed.

Sugar & Spice Popcorn

This sweet and spicy popcorn is refreshing and habit-forming!

3 tablespoons butter
2 tablespoons sugar
1/4 teaspoon nutmeg

1/2 teaspoon cinnamon
2 qts. popped popcorn

Melt butter over low heat. Add sugar and spices. Stir until sugar is dissovled. Drizzle over popcorn and toss to mix well. Makes 2 quarts.

Variation:
Other appropriate spices to use are allspice, anise, cloves, ginger, mint and pumpkin-pie spice.

Pink Party Popcorn

Or match the color of the popcorn to your decorating scheme.

3 tablespoons butter

1-1/2 cups miniature marshmallows

4 tablespoons strawberry-flavored gelatin

2 qts. popped popcorn

In a medium saucepan, melt butter over low heat. Stir marshmallows into the melting butter. Let them soften but not melt completely. Add the gelatin. Stir until butter-marshmallow mixture is evenly colored. Gelatin does not have to be dissolved. Drizzle over popcorn and mix well. Makes 2 quarts.

AN UNUSUAL GIFT

Popcorn-on-the-cob is an unusual, decorative and practical gift. Fill a basket with ears of popcorn, or fill up a shaker popper. Tie it with a ribbon and leave it on the doorstep or under the Christmas tree. You can grow your own popcorn-on-the-cob or buy it from specialty shops. Each ear yields 2 to 3 quarts of popped popcorn. Your gift will provide many happy hours of popping and snacking. Maybe they'll give you some.

Popcornology

WHY DOES POPCORN POP?

There was a time when some people thought a little devil lived inside each kernel of popcorn. Heating the kernel made him so mad that he burst the hull to escape. Modern scientific research has proved this superstition right! Except for the part about the devil.

Every popcorn kernel is like a little steam boiler. Inside, the starch grains hold small amounts of moisture. As the heat increases, the moisture turns to steam, but the hull prevents the steam from escaping. Enormous pressure builds up until finally the hull can stand it no longer. It shatters and the pressure is released so quickly that the inside of the kernel virtually explodes as it leaves its place of confinement. The grains of corn expand with the explosion and turn into the white flakes we know and love.

The moisture that escapes through the steam vents of your popper is the condensed steam that caused the kernels to explode

TYPES OF CORN

There is a common misconception that any kind of corn will pop if it is properly treated. This is not true. There are 5 main types of corn. Only popcorn really pops.

Sweet Corn—You find this type in grocery stores, either in the can or on the cob. The kernels are milky, sweet and just about everyone's favorite vegetable. Sweet corn will not pop at all.

Dent Corn or Field Corn—This is the most commonly grown type of corn in the U.S. It's used for livestock feed, making flour and cereals. It will sometimes pop feebly.

Flint Corn, or Indian Corn—This multi-colored ear is often used for decorations. It is a type of field corn grown mostly in South America. It will occasionally pop if the moisture level is just right.

Pod Corn—Also decorative, but not otherwise useful except for flower arrangements. It does not have a single husk as other corns do. Instead it has separate husks on each kernel.

Popcorn—Some people say it should really be called *popping corn*. It's hard while still on the ear, rather than becoming that way through some special process. Popcorn stalks, ears and kernels are usually smaller than other types of corn. Different hybrids are grown for different uses—for theaters, homes and for such specialized uses as making caramel corn.

POPPING EXPANSION

Popping expansion is one of the most noticeable and important characteristics of popcorn, and the easiest to measure. If one cup of kernels pops into 30 cups of popped corn, the popping expansion ratio is 30 to 1.

At the turn of the century the best popcorn had a popping ratio of about 15 to 1. Scientific breeding of hybrid corns has increased popping expansion. The best available popcorn today has an expansion ratio of over 40 to 1. The average is about 30 to 1.

The aim, of course, is not necessarily to try for the biggest popcorn possible, but for the popcorn that is the tenderest and tastiest. Fortunately, the largest pieces are also usually the crispiest and tenderest, and have the best flavor. It would seem logical that the best way to produce larger pieces would be to use larger kernels, but experiments have shown that the expansion volume decreases as the kernel grows larger. Small, short, round kernels expand the most because they contain a higher percentage of hard starch, which is the material that "explodes." In fact, during the processing of popcorn the larger kernels are taken out and sold for pigeon feed.

Popping expansion is affected by many factors including the variety of corn, the percentage of hard and soft starch in the kernel, the type of popped shape produced, the maturity and moisture content when harvested, and the handling

Almost everybody in the United States grew up with Cracker Jack® —including the sailor boy on the package, and his dog. Toys from the Cracker Jack® package bring back memories. The Ty Cobb baseball card was given away about 60 years ago. Most of us played with puzzles and whistles and opened each new package with eager anticipation.

during shelling and other processing. These are factors you have little control over.

Factors you *can* control include maintaining proper moisture level, selecting the best popping oil, and using the correct popping temperature. Popping expansion can sometimes be increased by as much as 50% by switching to a popper that operates at a higher temperature.

HULL-LESS POPCORN

The "enamel" or thin, hard covering around the kernel shatters when the kernel explodes. This hard covering is called the "hull." Most good popcorns are called *hull-less*, but this is a relative term. They have less hull than popcorns of years ago, but there is no such thing as an absolutely hulless popcorn. If there were, it wouldn't pop.

YELLOW AND WHITE POPCORN

The difference in color between yellow and white popcorn is obvious while they are still kernels, but less apparent after they are popped.

Yellow Popcorn has yellow kernels and the pieces appear white with a slight yellowish tinge. *White Popcorn* has white kernels and the popped corn is pure white.

Although yellow popcorn pops larger than white, some people feel that white popcorn is more tender and has a better flavor. Yellow popcorn is far more common than white, apparently because of its greater popping size. Only 10% of the popcorn grown in the United States is white.

White popcorn dominated the market until about 1935. Then, because of its acceptance by the theaters, yellow became more popular. Yellow popcorn looks more buttery, and it pops larger, so it is better liked by concessionaires selling popcorn by volume.

White popcorn is still popular in bars and cocktail lounges where volume is not an important consideration. It's usually well liked by people who consider themselves popcorn "cornnoisseurs."

Popcorn Balls, Bars & Crunches

YOUR FORTUNE IN A POPCORN BALL

Enliven your party or dinner with fortune-telling popcorn balls. Type unusual predictions on small slips of paper. Wrap the fortunes in plastic wrap or colored foil to keep them from getting smeared with syrup and mold them inside the popcorn balls.

HOW TO MAKE POPCORN BALLS

Have someone to work with when you make popcorn balls or other popcorn-syrup treats. One person makes the syrup while another pops the popcorn. One pours the syrup while another stirs the mixture. Forming the balls or bars goes much faster with 2 or more people working together. And speed is important to keep the syrup from hardening or overcooking.

One quart of popped popcorn makes 2 to 4 average-sized popcorn balls, depending on the amounts of other ingredients and how tightly they are packed together.

While the syrup is cooking, keep the popped popcorn warm in a large, 4-inch-deep, buttered pan. It's easier to mix ingredients in a circular pan about 8 inches in diameter than in a square or rectangular pan, but any shape will do as long as the pan is large enough to contain and mix the popcorn and syrup efficiently. The pan you roast your Thanksgiving turkey in will work very well. Popped popcorn will stay warm in a 250°F (121°C) oven. This step is not so much to keep the popcorn warm as to warm the pan holding the popcorn. Otherwise, the syrup will harden on contact with the pan.

Butter all surfaces that the syrup will contact. This includes the mixing container, which will be in the oven warming with the popcorn, your hands or rubber gloves, and the pan in which the balls, bars or crunches will cool or continue to cook.

Most syrups make the crunchiest popcorn balls when cooked to a temperature of 250°F (121°C) on a candy thermometer. Cooked to any tempera- ture above that, the cooled syrup will become very hard. An electric cooking pot with a thermostatic control is helpful because you can set it at the desired temperature.

If the syrup begins to smell as if it's burning, or it begins to smoke, immediately remove the syrup from the heat and pour it over the popcorn, even if it hasn't reached the desired temperature.

Wear rubber gloves to protect your hands against the hot ingredients while you are forming the popcorn balls. After putting on the gloves, slightly coat them with butter or oil. Some people use their bare hands, slightly wet or buttered. Try this method very cautiously so you won't burn your hands.

If you are working with large quantities of syrup, keep the syrup pan in hot water to prevent the syrup from hardening. If you keep it over the heat, the syrup may continue to cook and become too hard as it cools. If the syrup becomes too cool, place it over very low heat for just a few seconds.

Use as little pressure as possible as you form the balls. Press just enough so the shapes hold together. Try to pack the popcorn balls loosely. The looser they are, the easier to eat. You can make very chewy, easy to eat popcorn balls by loosely shaping the balls, then gently reshaping them as they cool. They may need to be shaped several times.

If the syrup is cooked to the point where the balls stay together the first time they are shaped, they probably will be hard and difficult to eat. If the syrup is cooked only to 250°F (121°C) it may be a few hours before the balls lose their stickiness.

Make sure the popcorn balls are completely dry before wrapping them.

DRESS-UP POPCORN BALLS

Add 1 to 2 cups of peanuts or other nuts—chopped or whole—to the popped popcorn and syrup before forming it into balls.

Tint the syrup with food coloring. Add the food coloring slowly, a drop at a time, to get just the right color. For special effects, tint each half of the syrup a different color. Arrange the different-colored balls in a basket or on a tray.

Make surprise balls by forming the popcorn-syrup mixture around a piece of candy, such as a malted-milk ball, a miniature candy bar or a marsh-mallow.

The popcorn ball or crunch recipes can also be used to make bars. Just pack the popcorn-syrup mixture in a lightly buttered, flat cake pan, 9" x 13" or larger. Cool, then cut into bars with a wet knife.

If you want a chocolate-dipped bar, chill the bars, dip into melted chocolate and chill again.

To make pie slices or wedges, turn the popcorn-syrup mixture into lightly buttered, flat pie plates. Spread it out evenly and let it cool. Cut into pie wedges with a wet knife.

Quickly pour syrup over popcorn, stirring as you pour. Mix well to coat the popcorn evenly.

With gloved hands, pick up a small amount of coated popcorn. Pack loosely into a ball. Each ball may have to be packed more than once.

REMOVE THE KERNELS

When making popcorn recipes such as balls, desserts, candies or other dishes where the popcorn is combined with other foods such as sugar, syrup and marshmallows, be certain that all unpopped kernels have been removed. Discovering a kernel in the middle of a popcorn ball is quite unpleasant.

Beginner's Popcorn Balls

A delicious, basic recipe. Don't forget to prepare your hands.

2 qts. popped popcorn
1 cup sugar
1/3 cup corn syrup
1/3 cup water

1/4 cup butter
1/4 teaspoon salt
1 teaspoon vanilla

Preheat oven to 250°F (121°C). Put popcorn in a large, 4-inch-deep, buttered baking pan. Keep warm in the oven. Combine sugar, corn syrup, water, butter and salt in a large saucepan. Stir over medium heat until sugar is dissolved. Cook until mixture reaches 250°F (121°C) on a candy thermometer, stirring frequently. Remove from heat. Quickly stir in vanilla. Remove popcorn from oven. Pour syrup mixture over popcorn, stirring to mix well. Form into balls. Makes approximately 8 balls.

Variations:
To make Spice Balls, substitute 1 tablespoon of powdered spice or crushed herbs for the vanilla.

To make Butterballs, increase the butter to 1/3 cup and increase the vanilla to 2 teaspoons. Add yellow food coloring.

Add a powdered, flavored ingredient, such as 1 tablespoon of instant-coffee powder, 2 tablespoons of instant-tea powder or 1/3 cup of non-dairy-creamer powder.

Simple Honey-Popcorn Balls

So simple and so good.

2 qts. popped popcorn
1-1/3 cups honey

Preheat oven to 250°F (121°C). Place popcorn in a large, 4-inch-deep-buttered, baking pan. Keep warm in oven. Heat honey until it reaches 250°F (121°C) on a candy thermometer. Remove popcorn from oven. Pour honey over popcorn. Allow to cool slightly. Shape popcorn into balls. Balls may remain a little sticky. Makes approximately 8 balls.

Variation:
Heat 1 cup honey and 1 cup sugar to 250°F (121°C) on a candy thermometer. Pour over popcorn. Cool. Shape into balls.

Rum-Flavored Popcorn Balls

A cozy evening's treat with steaming Cappucino or hot cocoa.

2 qts. popped popcorn
2/3 cup sugar
1/2 cup water
2-1/2 tablespoons light corn syrup

1 teaspoon salt
1 tablespoon rum flavor
1/3 teaspoon vinegar

Preheat oven to 250°F (121°C). Place popcorn in a large, 4-inch-deep, buttered baking pan. Keep warm in the oven. In a large saucepan, stir sugar, water and corn syrup together until sugar is dissolved. Boil without stirring until mixture reaches 250°F (121°C) on a candy thermometer. Remove from heat and quickly stir in salt, rum flavor and vinegar. Remove popcorn from oven. Pour syrup mixture over popcorn and mix thoroughly. Shape into balls. Makes approximately 8 balls.

Variation:
Substitute another flavor, such as almond extract or imitation banana extract, for rum flavor. Vary the amount, depending on your tastes and the strength of the flavor, extract or imitation extract.

Whiskey-Sour Popcorn Balls

If you don't like popcorn balls, try these. They'll change your mind.

2 qts. popped popcorn
Approximately 1/2 cup dry Whiskey-Sour mix
   (2 packets of individual-drink mix)
1/2 cup sugar

1/4 teaspoon salt
1/4 cup light corn syrup
1/2 cup water
1/2 teaspoon vinegar

Preheat oven to 250°F (121°C). Place popcorn in a large, 4-inch-deep, buttered baking pan. Keep warm in the oven. Combine other ingredients in a large saucepan. Cook until mixture reaches 250°F (121°C) on a candy thermometer. Remove popcorn from oven. Pour syrup mixture over popcorn. Mix well. Form into balls. Makes approximately 16 balls.

Variation:
Substitute another mix, such as Daiquiri or Mai-Tai for Whiskey-Sour mix.

Popcorn Pastels

For a dramatic effect, make 2 batches in contrasting colors.

4 qts. popped popcorn	1/2 teaspoon salt
1-1/2 cup granulated sugar	1/4 teaspoon cream of tartar
1/2 cup light corn syrup	3 to 4 tablespoons flavored gelatin powder
2 tablespoons butter	1 teaspoon baking soda

Preheat oven to 250°F (121°C). Place popcorn in a large, 4-inch-deep, buttered baking pan. Keep warm in oven. Cut 2 large pieces of wax paper to fit on 2 cooky sheets. Lightly butter the wax paper. In a larger saucepan combine the sugar, corn syrup, butter, salt and cream of tartar. Bring to a boil, stirring constantly. Cook, without stirring, until mixture reaches 250°F (121°C) on a candy thermometer. Stir in gelatin powder and continue cooking for about 1 minute until mixture reaches 260°F (126°C). Remove from heat. Stir in baking soda quickly but thoroughly. Remove popcorn from oven. Pour syrup mixture at once, while foamy, over popcorn. Mix gently to coat. Bake at 200°F (93°C) for 1 hour, stirring 2 or 3 times. Turn out on buttered wax paper. Cool completely. Separate into small pieces. Store in tightly covered containers. Makes 4 quarts.

Variation:
Use any flavor gelatin powder to match a holiday theme. Use red gelatin powder for Valentine's Day, green for St. Patrick's Day parties, and orange for Halloween.

Rainbow Popcorn Balls

Use colored miniature marshmallows for a rainbow effect.

2 qts. popped popcorn	2 cups colored miniature marshmallows
3 tablespoons butter	2 tablespoons flavored gelatin powder

Preheat oven to 250°F (121°C). Place popcorn in a large, 4-inch-deep, buttered baking pan. Keep warm in oven. In a medium saucepan, melt butter over low heat. Add marshmallows and stir until melted. Blend in gelatin powder. Remove popcorn from oven. Pour marshmallow mixture over popcorn, mixing well. Form into balls. Makes approximately 8 balls.

Marshmallow Confetti Balls

Make these gooey, colorful balls for a special occasion.

2 qts. popped popcorn
3 cups miniature marshmallows
1/3 cup butter

1/3 teaspoon vanilla
1/4 teaspoon salt
1 cup gum drops

Preheat oven to 250°F (121°C). Place popcorn in a large, 4-inch-deep baking pan. Keep warm in the oven. Melt marshmallows with butter over low heat, stirring occasionally, until smooth. Stir in vanilla and salt. Remove popcorn from oven. Combine with gum drops. Pour marshmallow-butter mixture over popcorn and gum drops. Toss until well coated. Form into balls. Makes approximately 8 balls.

Soft-Candy Popcorn Balls

Popcorn balls chock-full of familiar flavors.

2 qts. popped popcorn
1 cup sugar
1/3 cup dark or light corn syrup
1/3 cup water
1/4 cup butter

1/4 teaspoon salt
1 teaspoon vanilla
3 (1- to 2-oz.) pkgs. small, soft candies,
    such as Junior® Mints or M&M's®

Preheat oven to 250°F (121°C). Place popcorn in a large, 4-inch-deep, buttered baking pan. Keep warm in the oven. Place sugar, corn syrup, water, butter and salt in a large saucepan. Stir over medium heat until sugar is dissolved. Cook until mixture reaches 250°F (121°C) on a candy thermometer, stirring frequently. Remove from heat and quickly add vanilla. Remove popcorn from oven. Pour syrup over popcorn and stir to mix well. As mixture just begins to cool, sprinkle with candies and mix quickly and well. Form into balls. Makes approximately 8 balls.

Variation:
Mix half or more of the candy into the cooking syrup.

Russian-Tea Popcorn Balls

Try one. You'll go back for another.

2 qts. popped popcorn
1/2 cup sugar
1/2 cup powdered,
   orange breakfast-drink mix
1/6 cup instant tea powder
1/2 teaspoon cinnamon

1/4 teaspoon ground cloves
1/3 cup dark or light corn syrup
1/3 cup water
1/4 cup butter
1/4 teaspoon salt
1 teaspoon vanilla

Preheat oven to 250°F (121°C). Place popcorn in a large, 4-inch-deep, buttered baking pan. Keep warm in the oven. In a large saucepan, combine remaining ingredients except vanilla. Stir over medium heat until sugar is dissolved, then cook until mixture reaches 250°F (121°C) on a candy thermometer, stirring frequently. Remove from heat and quickly stir in vanilla. Remove popcorn from oven. Pour syrup mixture over popcorn, stirring to mix well. Form into balls. Makes approximately 8 balls.

Sweet & Sour Popcorn Balls

There's more than one way to take Vitamin C!

2 qts. popped popcorn
1/4 cup sugar
3/4 cup powdered,
   orange breakfast-drink mix
1/3 cup dark or light corn syrup

1/3 cup water
1/4 cup butter
1/4 teaspoon salt
1 teaspoon vanilla

Preheat oven to 250°F (121°C). Place popcorn in a large, 4-inch-deep, buttered baking pan. Keep warm in the oven. In a large saucepan, combine sugar, breakfast-drink mix, corn syrup, water, butter and salt. Stir over medium heat until sugar is dissolved. Cook until mixture reaches 250°F (121°C) on a candy thermometer, stirring frequently. Remove from heat and quickly stir in vanilla. Remove popcorn from oven. Pour syrup mixture over popcorn, stirring to mix well. Form into balls. Makes approximately 8 balls.

Variation:
Substitute powdered grape or grapefruit breakfast-drink mix for orange breakfast-drink mix.

Molasses-Peanut Popcorn Balls

Wrap a few and take to munch on at the movies.

2 qts. salted popped popcorn
2-1/2 cups salted peanuts
3/4 cup light molasses

3/4 cup light corn syrup
1 tablespoon vinegar
3 tablespoons butter

Preheat oven to 250°F (121°C). Mix popcorn and peanuts together in a large, 4-inch-deep, buttered baking pan. Keep warm in the oven. In a large saucepan, cook molasses, corn syrup and vinegar to 250°F (121°C) on a candy thermometer. Remove from heat, add butter and stir until butter melts. Remove popcorn and peanuts from oven. Pour syrup mixture slowly over popcorn and peanuts and stir until well coated. Shape into balls. Makes approximately 8 balls.

Hawaiian Popcorn Balls

Young and old will enjoy these on the patio with a cool drink.

2 qts. popped popcorn
2/3 cup sugar
1/2 cup water
2-1/2 tablespoons light corn syrup
1/8 teaspoon salt

1/3 teaspoon vinegar
1 teaspoon vanilla
1/2 cup shredded coconut
1/2 cup candied pineapple

Preheat oven to 250°F (121°C). Place popcorn in a large, 4-inch-deep, buttered baking pan. Keep warm in oven. In a large saucepan, combine sugar, water and corn syrup. Boil without stirring until mixture reaches 250°F (121°C) on a candy thermometer. Add salt and vinegar. Cook until mixture reaches 270°F (129°C). Remove from heat. Quickly stir in vanilla, coconut and pineapple. Remove popcorn from oven. Pour syrup mixture over popcorn. Mix well. Form into small balls. Makes approximately 15 balls.

Chocolate Popcorn Balls

What a combination! Popcorn in creamy, rich chocolate.

2 qts. popped popcorn
1-1/4 cups sugar
3/4 cup light corn syrup
1/2 cup unsweetened cocoa powder

1 teaspoon vinegar
1/8 teaspoon salt
2 tablespoons butter
1/4 cup evaporated milk

Preheat oven to 250°F (121°C). Place popcorn in a large, 4-inch-deep, buttered baking pan. Keep warm in the over. In a large saucepan, combine sugar, corn syrup, cocoa powder, vinegar and salt over medium heat. Add butter. Cook slowly, stirring constantly, until sugar dissolves. Bring to a boil. Add milk slowly so boiling does not stop. Cook over low heat, stirring occasionally, until mixture reaches 250°F (121°C) on a candy thermometer. Remove popcorn from oven. Pour syrup mixture over popcorn, mixing well. Dip out large spoonfuls and shape into small balls. Makes approximately 12 balls.

Candy-Bar Popcorn Balls

Recycle a candy bar to make these sweet and tasty balls.

2 qts. popped popcorn
3 (1- to 2-oz.-pkg.) candy bars
   such as Butterfinger® or Snickers®
3/4 cup sugar
1/3 cup dark or light corn syrup

1/3 cup water
1/4 cup butter
1/4 teaspoon salt
1 teaspoon vanilla

Preheat oven to 250°F (121°C). Put popcorn in a large, 4-inch-deep, buttered baking pan. Keep warm in oven. Place candy, sugar, corn syrup, water, butter and salt in a large saucepan. Stir over medium heat until candy and sugar are melted. Cook until mixture reaches 240°F (116°C) on a candy thermometer, stirring frequently. Remove from heat and quickly stir in vanilla. Remove popcorn from oven. Pour syrup mixture over popcorn and stir to mix well. Form into balls. Makes approximately 8 balls.

Variation:
Chop 1 (1 to 1-1/2 oz.) candy bar into small pieces and sprinkle over the syrup-popcorn mixture just before shaping into balls.

Gum-Drop Popcorn Balls

Sweet and chewy.

2 qts. salted popped popcorn
1 cup sugar
1/4 cup dark or light corn syrup

1/4 cup water
1/2 cup chopped gum drops

Preheat oven to 250°F (121°C). Place popcorn in a large, 4-inch-deep, buttered baking pan. Keep warm in oven. Cook sugar, corn syrup and water until mixture reaches 250°F (121°C) on a candy thermometer. Remove from heat and quickly stir in chopped gum drops. Remove popcorn from oven. Pour syrup mixture over popcorn and mix well. Form into balls. Makes approximately 8 balls.

Variations:
To make candied-Christmas-tree stand-ups, pack into a buttered, round pan and cut into wedges.

Peanut-Butter Popcorn Balls

Peanut-butter lovers of all ages will enjoy these.

2 qts. popped popcorn
1-1/2 cups light corn syrup

1-1/2 cups peanut butter

Preheat oven to 250°F (121°C). Place popcorn in a large, 4-inch-deep, buttered baking pan. Keep warm in the oven. In a large saucepan, boil syrup for 2 to 3 minutes. Slowly stir in peanut butter, until melted and well blended. Remove popcorn from oven. Pour over popcorn and mix well. Shape into 12 or more popcorn balls. Balls will not stick together well until the mixture starts to cool. They may have to be reshaped several times. Makes approximately 12 balls.

Variations:
Drop by the teaspoonful on waxed paper to make cookies. Let set until cool.
For a sweeter syrup, try 1 cup each, light corn syrup, sugar and peanut butter, boiling the sugar with the syrup.

Malted-Milk Popcorn Balls

This recipe brings an old favorite, malted milk, back into fashion.

2 qts. popped popcorn
1/3 cup malted-milk powder
3/4 cup sugar
1/3 cup dark or light corn syrup

1/3 cup water
1/4 cup butter
1/4 teaspoon salt
1 teaspoon vanillla

Preheat oven to 250°F (121°C). Place popcorn in large, 4-inch-deep, buttered baking pan. Keep warm in the oven. In a large saucepan, combine malted-milk powder, sugar, corn syrup, water, butter and salt. Cook over medium heat, stirring constantly, until sugar is dissolved. Then cook until mixture reaches 250°F (121°C) on a candy thermometer, stirring frequently. Remove from heat and quickly stir in vanilla. Remove popcorn from oven. Pour syrup mixture over popcorn, stirring to mix well. Form into popcorn balls. Makes approximately 8 balls.

Variation:
Form each popcorn ball around a chocolate-covered malted-milk ball.

Hard-Candy Popcorn Balls

Make chewy popcorn balls even chewier!

2 qts. popped popcorn
1 cup sugar
1/3 cup dark or light corn syrup
1/3 cup water
1/4 cup butter

1/4 teaspoon salt
3 to 4 (1-1/2-oz.) pkgs. small, hard candies
such as SweeTarts® or licorice bits,
divided into 2 equal parts
1 teaspoon vanilla

Preheat oven to 250°F (121°C). Place popcorn in a large, 4-inch-deep, buttered baking pan. Keep warm in the oven. Combine sugar, corn syrup, water, butter, salt and half of candy in a large saucepan. Stir over medium heat until sugar is dissolved. The candy need not be dissolved. Cook until mixture reaches 250°F (121°C) on a candy thermometer, stirring frequently. Remove from heat and quickly stir in vanilla. Remove popcorn from oven. Pour syrup over popcorn and stir to coat thoroughly. Sprinkle with remaining candies and mix well. Form into balls. Makes approximately 8 balls.

Candy-Stick Logs

Match the color of the wrappings to the flavors of the candy-sticks.

2 qts. popped popcorn
1-1/3 cups sugar
1 cup water
1/3 cup light corn syrup

2/3 teaspoon vinegar
1/3 teaspoon salt
1 teaspoon vanilla
8 (4-in.-long) candy sticks

Preheat oven to 250°F (121°C). Place popcorn in a large, 4-inch deep, buttered baking pan. Keep warm in the oven. Combine sugar, water, corn syrup, vinegar and salt in a large saucepan. Cook until mixture reaches 250°F (121°C) on a candy thermometer. Remove from heat and quickly stir in vanilla. Remove popcorn from oven. Pour syrup mixture over popcorn, stirring to mix well. Shape 1 cup of popcorn around each candy stick to form a log. Cool. If desired, wrap logs in colored cellophane or bright paper. Tie ends with ribbon. Makes 8 logs.

Fruit Goops

Better than the name suggests.

5 qts. popped popcorn
2 cups sugar
1 (6-oz.) can frozen grape juice
   concentrate

3/4 cup water
1/2 cup light corn syrup
1 teaspoon vinegar
1/2 teaspoon salt

Preheat oven to 250°F (121°C). Place popcorn in a large, 4-inch-deep, buttered baking pan. Keep warm in oven. Combine all ingredients except popcorn in a large saucepan. Bring to a boil. Lower heat and cook until mixture reaches 250°F (121°C) on a candy thermometer. Mixture will bubble, so watch closely to keep it from boiling over. Remove popcorn from oven. Pour syrup mixture slowly over hot popcorn and mix until well coated. Let stand several minutes. Form into balls. Makes approximately 24 balls.

Variation:
Substitute orange, sweetened lime or sweetened lemon-juice concentrate for grape-juice concentrate.

Add food coloring if more color is desired.

Cranberry Popcorn Balls

To make a holiday centerpiece, arrange these on a tray with fruit and tiny, gift-wrapped packages.

3 qts. popped popcorn
1-1/2 cups water
1 teaspoon whole cloves
1 teaspoon whole allspice
2 cinnamon sticks
1 cup chopped frozen cranberries, thawed

1-1/3 cups sugar
2 tablespoons light corn syrup
1 tablespoon shredded orange peel
1/4 teaspoon ground nutmeg
3 to 4 drops red food coloring

Preheat oven to 250°F (121°C). Place popcorn in a large, 4-inch-deep, buttered baking pan. Keep warm in the oven. Pour water into a large buttered saucepan. Securely tie cloves, allspice and cinnamon in a piece of cheesecloth and place in water. Cover saucepan and simmer for 20 minutes. Remove spices from pan. Stir in cranberries, sugar, corn syrup, orange peel, nutmeg and food coloring. Cook over medium heat, stirring constantly, until sugar is dissolved and mixture begins to boil. Continue cooking until mixture reaches 250°F (121°C) on a candy thermometer. Remove popcorn from oven. Pour syrup mixture slowly over popcorn, stirring to coat. Shape into balls. Makes approximately 12 balls.

Shoofly Snack

Here's that special Pennsylvania-Dutch richness.

2-1/2 qts. popped popcorn
1 cup peanuts, walnuts or pecans
1/2 cup butter
1 cup light-brown sugar, firmly packed
1/4 cup dark molasses

1/2 teaspoon salt
1/4 teaspoon cinnamon
1/4 teaspoon nutmeg
1 tablespoon water

Preheat oven to 250°F (121°C). Combine popcorn and nuts in a large, 4-inch-deep, buttered baking pan. Keep warm in the oven. Butter a 15-1/2" x 10-1/2" x 1" pan. In a large saucepan, melt butter. Stir in remaining ingredients. Cook over medium heat until boiling, stirring constantly. Boil until mixture reaches 260°F (126°C) on a candy thermometer. Remove popcorn and nuts from the oven. Slowly pour molasses glaze over popcorn and nuts, stirring to coat. Spread on the buttered pan. Bake for 20 minutes, stirring once. Cool and break or cut into pieces. Makes 2-1/2 quarts.

Baked Caramel Corn

This won't last long!

3 qts. popped popcorn
1/2 cup butter
1 cup brown sugar, firmly packed
1/4 cup dark or light corn syrup

1/2 teaspoon salt
1/4 teaspoon baking soda
1 teaspoon vanilla

Preheat oven to 250°F (121°C). Place popcorn in a large, 4-inch-deep, buttered baking pan. Keep warm in oven. Butter a 15-1/2" x 10-1/2" x 1" baking pan. In a large saucepan, melt butter over low heat. Stir in brown sugar, corn syrup and salt. Bring to a boil, stirring constantly. Boil without stirring for 5 minutes. Remove from heat and quickly stir in baking soda and vanilla. Remove popcorn from oven. Slowly pour syrup mixture over popcorn, mixing well. Turn into buttered baking pan. Bake for 1 hour, stirring every 15 minutes. Remove from oven. Cool completely. Break or cut apart. Store in a tightly covered container. Makes 3 quarts.

Variation:
Add 1 to 2 cups pecan halves, almonds or cashews before baking.

Coconut Munch

Exotic!

2-1/2 qts. popped popcorn
1/2 cup shredded coconut
1 (12-oz.) bottle orange soda

1/4 cup butter
1 cup sugar
1/2 cup light corn syrup

Preheat oven to 250°F (121°C). Place popcorn and coconut in large, 4-inch-deep, buttered baking pan. Keep warm in the oven. Butter a 15-1/2" x 10-1/2" x 1" baking pan. In a saucepan, combine orange soda, butter, sugar and corn syrup. Cook over medium heat, stirring until sugar dissolves. Boil mixture until it reaches 250°F (121°C) on a candy thermometer. Remove popcorn and coconut from oven. Slowly pour the orange glaze over the popcorn mixture, stirring until well coated. Spread in the buttered pan to cool. Break or cut into pieces to serve. Makes 2-1/2 quarts.

Peanut Butter & Jelly Popcorn Balls

Your youngsters will love 'em.

2 qts. popped popcorn   2/3 cup peanut butter
1 cup jelly

Preheat oven to 250°F (121°C). Place popcorn in a large, 4-inch-deep, buttered baking pan. Keep warm in oven. Melt the jelly and peanut butter in a large saucepan, mixing well. Bring to a boil for 1 minute. Remove popcorn from oven. Pour the peanut butter and jelly over the popcorn and mix to coat well. Pack each ball together and then place in a small cup or pudding dish. Place in the refrigerator. Form each ball again, if needed. Once cool, the balls will hold together. Wrap with plastic wrap and store in the refrigerator. Makes approximately 8 balls.

Oriental Crackle

A fanciful blend of tempting textures and flavors.

2-1/2 qts. popped popcorn   1/4 cup dark or light corn syrup
1/2 cup slivered almonds   1/2 teaspoon salt
1/2 cup shredded coconut   1/4 teaspoon baking soda
1/2 cup butter   3/4 cup chopped maraschino cherries
1 cup brown sugar, firmly packed

Preheat oven to 250°F (121°C). Place popcorn, almonds and coconut in a large, 4-inch-deep, buttered baking pan. Keep warm in the oven. Butter a 15-1/2" x 10-1/2" x 1" baking pan. Melt butter over low heat. Stir in brown sugar, corn syrup and salt. Bring to a boil, stirring constantly. Boil without stirring for 2 minutes. Remove from heat. Quickly stir in baking soda. Remove popcorn mixture from oven. Pour syrup mixture over popcorn mixture, stirring well. Spread on the buttered baking pan. Bake for 1 hour, stirring occasionally. Add cherries during the last 15 minutes of baking. Remove from oven. Cool completely. Break or cut apart and store in a tightly covered container. Makes 3 quarts.

Variation:
To make Pecan Crackle, leave out almonds and cherries. Add 1/2 cup pecan halves with the coconut. Add 1/2 teaspoon vanilla with baking soda.

Candy-Corn Crunch

Especially good for a Halloween treat.

2 qts. popped popcorn	1/4 cup water
2/3 cup brown sugar, firmly packed	1/4 cup butter
2/3 cup granulated sugar	3/4 teaspoon salt
1/2 cup dark corn syrup	3/4 cup candy corn

Preheat oven to 250°F (121°C). Place popcorn in a large, 4-inch-deep, buttered baking pan. Keep warm in oven. Butter 2 cooky sheets. In a large saucepan, mix sugars, corn syrup, water, butter and salt. Heat slowly to boiling, stirring to dissolve sugar. Cook until mixture reaches 250°F (121°C). Remove popcorn from oven. Pour syrup over popcorn. Stir well to coat each piece. Sprinkle candy corn over the mixture and stir quickly. Spread out on buttered cooky sheets. Cool. Break or cut apart. Makes 2-1/2 quarts.

Cherry Puffs

George Washington's favorite.

4 tablespoons butter	4-1/2 cups miniature marshmallows
2 qts. hot, popped popcorn	4 tablespoons chopped maraschino cherries

Preheat oven to 300°F (149°C). Cut large pieces of wax paper to fit 2 cooky sheets. Lightly butter wax paper. Melt butter over low heat. Place hot popcorn in a large, 4-inch-deep baking pan and spread marshmallows over the top. Heat oven until marshmallows are almost completely melted. Remove from oven. Quickly add cherries and melted butter. Toss until well mixed. Place by heaping tablespoonfuls on wax paper and shape into small balls. Make approximately 20 balls.

Honey Crunch

This won't stay in the bowl very long!

3 qts. popped popcorn	1/2 cup butter
1 cup nuts	1/2 cup honey, room temperature

Preheat oven to 250°F (121°C). Place popcorn and nuts in a large, 4-inch-deep baking pan. Keep warm in oven. Lightly butter a cooky sheet. Melt butter over low heat. Blend in honey until well mixed. Remove popcorn mixture from oven. Set oven at 350°F (177°C). Pour butter-honey mixture over popcorn-nut mixture and mix well. Spread in thin layer on cooky sheet. Bake 10 to 15 minutes or until crisp. When cool break or cut apart. Makes 3-1/4 quarts.

Cobblestone Crisp

An elegant way to enjoy popcorn.

2-1/2 qts. popped popcorn
1/4 cup butter
1 cup light corn syrup
1 cup sugar

1/2 teaspoon salt
1 teaspoon vanilla
1 cup chopped candied cherries, or
    mixed candied fruit

Preheat oven to 250°F (121°C). Place popcorn in a large, 4-inch-deep, buttered baking pan. Keep warm in the oven. Butter a 15-1/2" x 10-1/2" x 1" baking pan. In a large saucepan, melt butter, coating sides of the pan. Add corn syrup, sugar and salt. Cook over medium heat, stirring occasionally, until mixture reaches 250°F (121°C) on a candy thermometer. Remove from heat and quickly stir in vanilla. Remove popcorn from oven. Mix immediately with candied fruit. Pour hot syrup slowly over popcorn and fruit, tossing to coat. Spread on the buttered baking pan. When completely cool, break or cut into pieces. Makes 3 quarts.

Chocolate Clusters

Chewy, sweet, crunchy, nutritious—all in a cluster!

2 tablespoons milk
1 tablespoon butter
24 chocolate caramels
    (approximately 1-1/2 cups)
8 vanilla caramels
    (approximately 1/2 cup)

1/4 teaspoon salt
1/2 cup coarsely chopped,
    dry-roasted cashew nuts
1 qt. popped popcorn
1 cup granola
1/2 cup raisins

Preheat oven to 200°F (93°C). Combine milk, butter, chocolate and vanilla caramels and salt in the top of a double boiler. Melt over hot water, stirring until smooth and creamy. In a large bowl, combine nuts, popcorn, granola, and raisins. Add melted-chocolate mixture and mix thoroughly. Drop by teaspoonfuls on ungreased cookie sheet. Bake for 15 minutes. Allow to cool completely before removing from pan. Makes approximately 30 clusters.

Sister Mabel's Caramel Corn

This caramel corn, packed in a brightly colored canister, makes a delightful gift.

6 qts. popped popcorn
2 cups light-brown sugar,
   firmly packed
1/2 cup light corn syrup

1/2 lb. butter or margarine
1/4 teaspoon cream of tartar
1 teaspoon salt
1 teaspoon baking soda

Preheat oven to 250°F (121°C). Place popcorn in a large, 4-inch-deep, buttered baking pan. Keep warm in oven. Cut large pieces of wax paper to fit cooky sheet. Lightly butter the wax paper. In a large saucepan, combine brown sugar, corn syrup, butter, cream of tartar and salt. Bring to a boil over medium-high heat, stirring constantly. Continue to stir constantly and boil rapidly until mixture reaches 260°F (127°C) on a candy thermometer, about 5 minutes. Remove from heat. Stir in baking soda quickly but thoroughly. Remove popcorn from oven. Pour syrup mixture over popcorn. Stir gently until well coated. Bake at 200°F (93°C) for 1 hour, stirring 2 or 3 times during baking. Turn out at once on wax paper. Spread out and allow to cool completely. Break or cut apart. Store in a tightly covered container. Makes 6 quarts.

Chocolaty Popcorn Squares

Sweet, crunchy and topped with melted chocolate.

2 qts. popped popcorn
1-1/3 cups chopped peanuts
2 cups shredded coconut
2 cups sugar
2/3 cup dark corn syrup

2/3 cup water
2-1/2 tablespoons butter
1-1/3 teaspoons vanilla
2/3 cup milk-chocolate cooking chips

Preheat oven to 250°F (121°C). Place popcorn, peanuts and coconut in a large, 4-inch-deep, buttered baking pan. Butter a 13" x 9" baking pan. Combine sugar, corn syrup and water in a large saucepan. Cook and stir until the sugar dissolves. Cook without stirring until mixture reaches 250°F (121°C) on a candy thermometer. Remove from heat. Quickly stir in butter and vanilla. Remove popcorn mixture from oven. Pour syrup over popcorn mixture, stirring well. Press into the buttered baking pan and immediately cut into 1-1/2-inch squares. Cut again as it cools. In a small saucepan, melt the chocolate cooking chips in a double boiler over hot water. Drizzle over the top of squares. Makes 48 squares.

Praline Crunch

Popcorn gives new crunch to a traditional candy.

2 qts. popped popcorn
1 (5-oz.) pkg. coconut-pecan frosting mix
1/4 cup butter
2 tablespoons light corn syrup

1/4 cup water
1/2 teaspoon rum flavoring
1/4 teaspoon salt
1/4 teaspoon baking soda

Preheat oven to 200°F (93°C). Place popcorn in a large, 4-inch-deep, buttered baking dish. Keep warm in the oven. Combine frosting mix, butter, corn syrup, water, rum flavoring and salt. Heat until mixture begins to boil, stirring occasionally. Remove from heat. Stir in baking soda until the mixture foams. Remove popcorn from oven. Pour syrup mixture over popcorn and stir until all is well coated. Bake 1 hour, stirring every 15 minutes. Cool. Break or cut apart. Makes 2 quarts.

Root-Beer Crunch

A rare and tasty blend of old-fashioned flavors.

2 qts. popped popcorn
1 cup salted pecans
1 (12-oz.) bottle root beer
1 cup sugar

1/2 cup light corn syrup
1/2 cup butter
1/4 teaspoon salt

Preheat oven to 250°F (121°C). Combine popcorn and pecans in a large, 4-inch-deep, buttered baking pan. Keep warm in the oven. Butter 2 cooky sheets. Pour root beer slowly down the side of a large saucepan. Add sugar, corn syrup, butter and salt. Stir gently, but well. Bring to a boil, stirring until sugar melts. Cook until mixture reaches 250°F (121°C) on a candy thermometer. Remove popcorn and pecans from oven. Pour syrup mixture over popcorn and pecans. Mix well. Spread on buttered cooky sheets and separate into pieces. Cool and serve. Makes 2-1/4 quarts.

Variation:
Substitute a cola, uncola or other soft drink for root beer.

Peanut-Butter Nougat Bars

Creamy-sweet, chocolate-laced and crunchy, too!

2-1/2 qts. popped popcorn
1 cup granola
1 cup butterscotch cooking chips
1/3 cup peanut butter

2 tablespoons butter or margarine
3 cups miniature marshmallows
1/4 teaspoon salt
1 cup semi-sweet chocolate cooking chips

Preheat oven to 250°F (121°C). Butter a 9" x 13" pan. Mix popcorn and granola in the buttered pan. Keep warm in the oven. Combine the butterscotch cooking chips, peanut butter, butter, marshmallows and salt in the top part of a double boiler over hot water. Stir constantly until melted and smooth. Remove popcorn and granola from oven. Pour marshmallow mixture over popcorn and granola. Toss until well mixed. Press smoothly in pan. Melt the chocolate cooking chips over hot, not boiling, water. Drizzle over the nougat mixture to form a lacy pattern. Cool until firm. Cut into 1" x 2" bars. Makes 54 bars.

©1975 Hunt-Wesson Foods, Inc., Orville Redenbacher Gourmet® Popping Corn—used by permission.

Molasses Crunch

The aroma brings back memories of Grandmother's kitchen.

2 qts. popped popcorn
2 cups whole or chopped nuts
1-1/3 cups molasses
1 cup sugar
2 tablespoons butter

1 tablespoon vinegar
2/3 cup water
1/4 teaspoon baking soda
1 teaspoon vanilla

Preheat oven to 250° (121°C). Combine popcorn and nuts in a large, 4-inch-deep, buttered baking pan. Keep warm in the oven. Butter two 8-inch-square baking pans. Mix molasses, sugar, butter, vinegar and water. Cook slowly without stirring, until mixture reaches 250°F (121°C) on a candy thermometer. Add baking soda and stir well. Remove from heat and quickly stir in vanilla. Remove popcorn and nuts from oven. Pour syrup mixture over popcorn and nuts and mix well. Pour into buttered pans. Cut when cool. Makes 24 squares.

Honey Popcorn Balls

A real sweet-tooth satisfier.

3 qts. slightly salted popped popcorn
3/4 cup honey
1-1/4 cups light corn syrup
1 tablespoon butter

1/2 tablespoon vinegar
1 teaspoon salt
1/2 teaspoon vanilla

Preheat oven to 250°F (121°C). Place salted popcorn in a large, 4-inch-deep, buttered baking pan. Keep warm in the oven. In a large saucepan, boil honey, corn syrup, butter, vinegar and salt, stirring occasionally, then frequently as mixture approaches 275°F (135°C) on a candy thermometer. Remove from heat and quickly stir in vanilla. Remove popcorn from oven. Pour syrup mixture over popcorn and mix well. Shape into balls. Makes approximately 15 balls.

Chocolate Popcorn

Good for breakfast, too.

3 qts. popped popcorn
2-1/2 cups semi-sweet chocolate
    cooking chips (1-1/4 pkgs.)

2/3 cup light corn syrup

Preheat oven to 250°F (121°C). Place popcorn in a large, 4-inch-deep, buttered baking dish. Keep warm in the oven. Lightly butter 2 cooky sheets or large pieces of wax paper. In the top of a double boiler over hot water, melt chocolate and stir in corn syrup. Remove popcorn from oven. Pour syrup mixture over popcorn, stirring to mix well. Spread on cooky sheets or wax paper. Separate the pieces. Cool before serving. Makes 3 quarts.

Variations:
Cover a handful with milk and serve instead of cereal for breakfast.

For a milder chocolate taste, substitute milk-chocolate cooking chips for the semi-sweet chocolate cooking chips.

Spearmint Crackle

Spearmint surprises in every bite.

2 qts. popped popcorn
3 tablespoons butter
1/2 cup sugar
1/4 cup light corn syrup

3 tablespoons water
1-1/2 cups chopped spearmint-leaf candies
2 to 5 drops green food coloring,
   if desired

Preheat oven to 250°F (121°C). Place popcorn in a large, 4-inch-deep, buttered baking pan. Keep popcorn warm in the oven. Lightly butter a 15-1/2" x 10-1/2" x 1" pan. In a large saucepan, combine butter, sugar, corn syrup, water and spearmint-leaf candies. Cook over medium heat until boiling, stirring constantly. Continue to boil mixture, stirring occasionally, until it reaches 260°F (126°C) on a candy thermometer. The spearmint candies will not melt completely. Add food coloring, if desired. Remove popcorn from oven. Pour syrup over popcorn, stirring until all is evenly coated. Spread on buttered pan to cool. Break or cut into pieces. Makes 2 quarts.

Nature Crunch

Delicious and only moderately sweet.

2 qts. popped popcorn
1 cup peanuts
1 cup wheat germ
1/4 cup butter
1 cup sugar

1/3 cup honey
1/3 cup water
1/2 teaspoon salt
1 cup raisins

Preheat oven to 250°F (121°C). Mix popcorn, peanuts and wheat germ in a large, 4-inch-deep, buttered baking pan. Keep warm in the oven. Butter 2 large, 2-inch-deep baking pans. In a large saucepan melt butter. Stir in sugar, honey, water and salt. Cook over medium heat, stirring constantly, until sugar is dissolved and mixture starts to boil. Cook until mixture reaches 250°F (121°C) on a candy thermometer. Remove popcorn mixture from oven. Stir in raisins. Pour syrup mixture slowly over popcorn mixture, stirring to coat. Spread 1-inch deep in the buttered baking pans. Bake for 45 minutes, stirring occasionally. Cool. Break or cut apart. Makes 3 quarts.

Coconut-Caramel Popcorn

A superb combination for coconut fans and popcorn lovers.

2 qts. popped popcorn
2/3 cup shredded coconut
1-1/3 cup brown sugar, firmly packed

1/3 cup water
2 teaspoons butter
1/6 teaspoon baking soda

Preheat oven to 250°F (121°C). Place popcorn and coconut in large baking pan and keep warm in the oven. Butter a 15-1/2" x 10-1/2" x 1" baking pan. In a large saucepan, bring brown sugar, water and butter to a boil, stirring occasionally. Boil until mixture reaches 250°F (121°C) on a candy thermometer. Remove from heat and quickly stir in baking soda. Remove popcorn and coconut from oven. While syrup is still foamy, stir in popcorn and coconut until well coated. Spread in the buttered baking pan. When completely cool, break or cut into pieces. Makes 2 quarts.

Peanut Butter 'N Jelly Bar

Watch this become a favorite after-school treat.

2 qts. popped popcorn
1/4 cup dark or light corn syrup
1-1/4 cup crunchy peanut butter

3/4 cup marshmallow creme
1/2 cup jelly or jam
1/2 cup chopped nuts

Preheat oven to 250°F (121°C). Place popcorn in a large, 4-inch-deep, buttered baking pan. Keep warm in the oven. Butter a 9" x 13" baking pan. Combine corn syrup, peanut butter and marshmallow creme in the top of a double boiler. Heat, stirring until mixture is blended. Remove popcorn from oven. Pour syrup mixture over popcorn and mix thoroughly. Spread half of mixture in buttered baking pan. Cover with jelly or jam. Top with remaining popcorn mixture. Sprinkle with chopped nuts. Cut into bars. Chill and cut again. Makes 12 to 16 bars.

Breakfasts

WHO EATS POPCORN FOR BREAKFAST?

Colonial housewives put popcorn to work at mealtime. Served with sugar and cream, popcorn became the first puffed cereal, a use almost forgotten now.

Eating popcorn for breakfast may seem strange at first. Try it, like the colonists did, covered with milk or cream. Because popcorn and milk are naturally sweet, you'll need little, if any, sugar or honey. If you like, add berries, raisins or sliced bananas. Some of the sugared recipes in the Sweet-Snacks section make a delicious cereal. Try Sugar-Coated Popcorn, page 50, or Sugar & Spice Popcorn, page 50.

If you are frying bacon or sausage, brown a generous handful of popped popcorn in the pan before removing the bacon or sausage. Served with the bacon or sausage, the browned popcorn adds a delicious nutty flavor.

Keep a small supply of unbuttered popcorn in a tightly covered container. If you don't have time to prepare your usual breakfast, a bowl of this popcorn and a can of vegetable juice will hold you until lunch.

Because popcorn tends to absorb liquids, many of the recipes in this section should not be prepared until just before serving. After 30 minutes or so the crunchiness of the popcorn and most of the appeal of the breakfast item may be lost.

GROUND POPCORN

Some of the recipes in this section call for ground popped popcorn. It's easy to grind popcorn in a blender or food processor. See the section on Ground Popcorn, page 96.

Granola

Serve for breakfast with milk or cream, or as a snack anytime.

1/2 cup smooth or crunchy peanut butter
1 tablespoon vegetable oil
1 tablespoon water
2 teaspoons vanilla
1/2 cup honey
1/4 cup brown sugar, firmly packed
1/2 teaspoon salt

2 cups uncooked oats
2 cups wheat germ
2 cups medium-ground, popped popcorn
1 cup sesame seeds
1 cup shredded coconut
1/2 to 1 cup raisins or chopped dried fruit,
   if desired

Preheat oven to 300°F (149°C). Blend peanut butter, oil, water, vanilla, honey, brown sugar and salt in a bowl and set aside. In a large, 4-inch deep baking pan, mix together oats, wheat germ, ground popcorn, sesame seeds and coconut. Add peanut-butter mixture, stirring to coat. Bake for 40 to 45 minutes, stirring after 20 minutes. Remove from oven and add raisins or dried fruit, if desired. Cool and store in a covered container. Makes 2 to 3 quarts.

Popcornmeal Cereal

Cooked popcorn cereal? Why not?

2 qts. popped popcorn
2 cups boiling water

1/2 teaspoon salt
2 to 3 cups warm milk or cream

Stir popcorn into boiling water. Add salt. Boil at least 5 minutes, stirring occasionally. Remove from heat, cover pan, and let stand several minutes. Serve with warm milk or cream. Makes 4 servings.

Variations:
Popcornmeal is naturally sweet, but may be topped with brown sugar, cinnamon, honey, raisins or fruit, if desired.

Use ground popped popcorn in place of whole popped popcorn.

Omelet

A thrifty way to flavor eggs.

1 cup medium-ground, popped popcorn	Pinch of paprika
1/4 cup milk	1 teaspoon chopped parsley
2 eggs, well beaten	1 tablespoon butter
1/2 teaspoon salt	1/4 cup grated cheese

In a medium bowl, add ground popcorn to milk, and allow it to soak 3 to 5 minutes. Stir in eggs, salt, paprika and parsley. Melt butter in an omelet pan. Pour in the popcorn-egg mixture. Cook on moderate heat. Add cheese on top of omelet just before omelet becomes firm. Fold and turn out on platter. Makes 2 servings.

Scrapple

A versatile, filling breakfast treat.

1/2 cup yellow cornmeal	1-1/2 cups boiling water
1/2 teaspoon salt	1/2 cup hominy grits
1/2 cup cold water	1/2 cup medium-ground, popped popcorn

Mix cornmeal, salt, and cold water. Pour gradually into boiling water, stirring constantly. Allow to return to a boil, then slowly add hominy grits and ground popcorn. Reduce heat and cover. Continue cooking over low heat for 5 to 7 minutes, stirring frequently. Place in cereal bowls and serve with milk or cream. Add fruit, if desired. Makes 4 servings.

Variations:

Fry in a buttered frying pan for 3 to 5 minutes. Serve with bacon, sausage or ham.

Fry for 3 to 5 minutes in a buttered frying pan with chopped chili peppers or pre-cooked sausage, bacon or ham.

Mix in 2 to 4 tablespoons of milk and fry like a large pancake. It may crumble in the pan. Serve with syrup.

Honey-Frosted Flakes

Naturally sweet and nutritious.

1 qt. popped popcorn
1/2 cup raisins
1/2 cup honey

2 to 3 cups milk or cream
Fruit, if desired

Preheat oven to 250°F (121°C). Butter a cooky sheet. Mix popcorn and raisins together and spread in a large, 4-inch-deep, buttered baking pan. Keep warm in oven. Boil honey several minutes, being careful to not let it burn. Remove popcorn from oven. While honey is still foamy, pour over popcorn and raisins, mixing thoroughly. Spread out on cooky sheet and separate into individual pieces if possible. After completely cool, store in a covered container. Use just like any other dry cereal. Serve covered with milk or cream and topped with fruit, if desired. Makes 4 to 6 servings.

Toasted Popcorn Flakes

Be the first in your neighborhood to enjoy the new breakfast fad.

1 tablespoon butter
1 qt. popped popcorn

2 to 3 cups milk or cream

Preheat oven to 400°F (204°C). Melt butter over low heat. Drizzle over the popcorn. Place in the oven on a cooky sheet until crisp and slightly brown, approximately 5 minutes. Pour into cereal bowls and cover with milk or cream. Makes 4 servings.

Variations:
Top with brown sugar, cinnamon, honey, raisins or fruit, if desired. Popcorn covered with milk is naturally sweet.

To make Popcorn Toast, use 1/2 tablespoon of butter to brown popcorn in the oven. Pour other 1/2 tablespoon over popcorn after it browns. Salt lightly and serve.

Overnight Popcornmeal Cereal

A tasty and filling breakfast.

2 qts. popped popcorn
2 cups water

2 cups milk
1-1/2 to 2 cups warm milk or cream

In a large pan, pour water over popcorn. Stir. Let soak overnight. In the morning, cover with milk and warm for about 5 minutes on medium heat. Do not boil. Serve with warm milk or cream. Makes 4 servings.

Variations:
Top with brown sugar, cinnamon, honey, raisins or fruit, if desired. Popcorn covered with milk is naturally sweet.

Pancakes

A subtle change in the pancake routine.

1 cup pancake mix
2/3 cup milk
1 egg

1 tablespoon vegetable oil
3/4 cup medium or
    finely ground, popped popcorn

In a large bowl, mix all ingredients together. Drop on 375°F (190°C) griddle by 1/4 cupfuls. Cook until bubbles form on top. Turn and brown. Makes approximately ten 4-inch pancakes.

Popcorn Milk

A filling, naturally sweet, breakfast drink.

1 to 1-1/4 cups cold milk
2 heaping tablespoons finely ground,
  popped popcorn, popped in as little oil as necessary

Pour milk into a large glass. Stir ground popcorn into milk. You don't need to add sugar or honey. Makes 1 serving.

Appetizers & Light Fare

COMPANY'S COMING

Company's coming and you're all out of chips and crackers! Use large pieces of buttered and salted popcorn to scoop dips or to accompany fondues. Or try a new and interesting appetizer from this recipe section. How about crusty Battered Mushrooms or crisp Toasted Zucchini?

Use plain or buttered popped popcorn as soup croutons. Popcorn croutons are especially tasty in pea soup or corn soup. For a toasted flavor, roast the popped popcorn in a 300°F (149°C) oven for 3 to 5 minutes before floating them in the soup. Toss a handful of popped popcorn into your bowl of beans or chili. Popcorn generously buttered and sprinkled with Parmesan cheese is especially good as a side dish with chili.

One editor drops a few pieces of popped popcorn into his salad bowl after finishing his salad. The popcorn absorbs the zesty flavors of the salad dressing left in the bottom of the bowl. It's a fun and thrifty way to finish leftover salad dressing.

On a hot evening, when you feel like a light meal, serve a refreshing green salad, ice-cold milk and hot, freshly popped and buttered popcorn. If you prefer even more flavor in your light meal, try one of the popcorn recipes included in the section on Salty Snacks, pages 36 to 47.

If you're trying to cut down on second helpings and large, gooey desserts, dull your appetite 30 minutes before mealtime with a cup of unbuttered popcorn. One cup of unbuttered popped popcorn contains 25 to 55 calories, depending on the size of the pieces of popcorn. Because small pieces of popcorn fit closer together than large ones, there will be more small pieces, and therefore more calories, in 1 cup.

Because popcorn absorbs liquids, many of the recipes in this section should not be prepared until immediately before serving. The crunchiness of the popcorn and most of the appeal of the food item may be lost after sitting on the platter or in the bowl for 30 minutes.

Popcorn Crepe Batter

Here's a new and delicious crepe batter.

2 eggs
3/4 cup flour
1/4 teaspoon salt

1/2 cup finely ground, popped popcorn
1-1/4 cups milk

Mix ingredients until smooth, then refrigerate for at least 1 hour. Remove from refrigerator and stir batter. Cook crepes on upside-down crepe griddle or in traditional pan. Makes 18 to 22 crepes.

Hush Puppies

Of course, you'll serve them with fish.

2 cups finely ground, popped popcorn
1 egg
1 tablespoon flour
1/2 teaspoon salt
1-1/2 teaspoons baking powder

1/4 teaspoon black pepper
1 medium onion, finely chopped
1/2 cup or less milk
Vegetable oil used for frying fish

Stir all ingredients together, using just enough milk to make a thick paste. Fry in hot 375°F (190°C) oil by the large tablespoonful. Serve while hot. Makes 12 to 15 hush puppies.

Garlic Croutons

Just a delicate touch of garlic to blend with your soup.

1 garlic clove
2 tablespoons butter

1 qt. popped popcorn

In a small skillet, melt butter over low heat. Chop garlic. Add to melting butter. Simmer over low heat for 3 to 5 minutes. Remove garlic pieces. Drizzle butter over popcorn. Store leftover croutons in an airtight container for several days. Makes 1 quart.

Battered Mushrooms

If you make these once, you'll make them again and again.

1/2 cup finely ground, popped popcorn
2 teaspoons salt
1 teaspoon paprika
1 teaspoon pepper

1 egg
2 (4-oz.) cans whole mushrooms or
   1/2 lb. fresh mushroom caps
1 cup or less vegetable oil

Mix ground popcorn, salt, paprika and pepper. Set aside. Beat egg. Dip mushrooms in egg and roll in popcorn mixture. Fry for 3 to 5 minutes in hot oil. Serve while hot. Makes 6 servings. •

Chocolate Fondue

Don't be afraid to use your fingers.

2 squares unsweetened chocolate
6 tablespoons water
1 cup sugar
Dash of salt

3 tablespoons butter
1/4 teaspoon vanilla
2 to 3 qts. popped popcorn,
   plain or buttered

Melt chocolate with water over low heat, stirring until smooth. Add sugar and salt. Cook and stir until smooth and slightly thickened. Stir in butter and vanilla until smooth. Keep warm in chafing dish or on warmer. Carefully dip popcorn into chocolate with your fingers. Makes approximately 1 cup.

Toasted Zucchini

Vegetables take on an interesting new flavor.

2 medium zucchini
2 to 3 cups finely ground, popped popcorn

1 cup vegetable oil
2 eggs, beaten

Cut zucchini into 1/8-inch slices. Place ground popcorn in a large bowl. Heat oil in a large skillet over medium heat. Dip zucchini slices in egg, then in ground popcorn. Cook in hot oil until golden. Serve piping hot. Makes 4 to 6 servings.

Cheese Fondue

A nippy party treat.

1 (8-oz.) jar processed cheese spread
3 tablespoons chopped green chilies
Dash of onion salt

2 to 3 qts. popped popcorn,
    buttered and salted

Melt cheese over low heat. Add chilies and onion salt. Keep warm in chafing dish or on warmer. Dip with popcorn. Makes approximately 1 cup.

Waldorf Salad

Serve this bright and tasty salad on lettuce leaves.

1/2 cup grated carrots
1/2 cup chopped pineapple
1/2 cup raisins
1/2 cup nuts

1/2 cup chopped celery
1/2 cup chopped apples
1 to 1-1/2 tablespoons mayonaise
1/2 cup medium-ground, popped popcorn

Mix all ingredients except ground popcorn together. Just before serving stir in the ground popcorn. Makes 4 servings.

Banana Popcorn Salad

A light refreshing lunch for a hot day.

1 banana
2 lettuce leaves

2 tablespoons salad dressing
2 tablespoons medium-ground, popped popcorn

Cut banana in half lengthwise and place each half on lettuce leaf. Cover with salad dressing. Sprinkle with ground popcorn. Makes 2 servings.

Pepper Spread

Can they guess what the ingredients are?

1 cup finely ground, popped popcorn
1/2 cup finely chopped red and green
   peppers or pickles

1 tablespoon sour cream
Salt to taste

Mix all ingredients well and chill. Spread on crackers. Makes spread for 16 crackers or filling for 2 sandwiches.

Savory Cheese Spread

Company coming? Nothing fancy to serve? Just mix this up.

1 cup finely ground, popped popcorn
1 cup grated cheese
1 teaspoon mayonnaise

Salt to taste
Paprika to taste
Olive slices, if desired

Mix ingredients well and chill. Spread on crackers. Top with olive slices, if desired. Makes spread for 16 crackers or filling for 2 sandwiches.

Vegetable-Salad Sandwich

A meal in a sandwich.

3/4 cup finely ground, popped popcorn
1/2 cup finely shredded carrot
1/8 cup finely chopped celery
1/8 cup mayonnaise

2 tablespoons peanut butter
4 slices bread
2 lettuce leaves
2 teaspoons mayonnaise

Combine ground popcorn, carrot, celery and mayonnaise. Spread peanut butter on 2 slices of bread. Top with ground-popcorn mixture, lettuce and remaining slices of bread. Spread with mayonnaise. Makes filling for 2 sandwiches or spread for 16 crackers.

Egg-Sardine Spread

Like Sardines? This is for you!

2 hard-boiled eggs, finely chopped
1/4 cup finely ground, popped popcorn

1 (3-3/4-oz.) can sardines, drained
1 teaspoon or more lemon juice to moisten

Combine eggs, ground popcorn and sardines. Moisten with lemon juice. Mix thoroughly, making a thick paste. Chill. Serve on rounds of toast or on crackers. Makes spread for 40 crackers or filling for 5 sandwiches.

Olive Spread

You won't have to add salt to this one.

2 tablespoons chopped green olives,
   or 4 tablespoons chopped black olives

2 cups finely ground, popped popcorn
2 heaping tablespoons sour cream

Mix olives, ground popcorn and sour cream together. Spread on crackers. Makes spread for 16 crackers or filling for 2 sandwiches.

Cheese Spread

Ground popcorn changes the flavor.

1 (8-oz.) pkg. cream cheese
1 cup finely ground, popped popcorn

1/2 cup chopped pickles or
   olives, drained

Let cheese soften to room temperature. Make a paste of the cheese and ground popcorn. Stir in pickles or olives. Spread on crackers or bread. Makes filling for 5 sandwiches or spread for 40 crackers.

Variation:
Substitute raisins, berries or chopped figs for pickles or olives.

Potato Salad

Surprisingly good! Try it.

4 medium-sized white potatoes
2 celery hearts, chopped
2-1/2 cups medium-ground, popped popcorn
Salt and pepper to taste

1 cup mayonnaise
Lettuce leaves
1 cup cream

Boil potatoes and cut into thin slices. Add celery, ground popcorn, salt and pepper to taste. Stir in mayonnaise. Place on lettuce leaves. Cover with cream and serve immediately. Makes 4 to 6 servings.

Variation:
Top with sour cream in place of cream.

Daphne's Hors d'Oeuvres

What gives it that nutty flavor?

1 (3-oz.) pkg. cream cheese
1 cup finely ground popcorn

40 small crackers or bread squares
20 dates, pitted and halved

Let cheese soften to room temperature. Mix ground popcorn and cream cheese together to form a paste. Spread on crackers or bread. Top with a halved date. Makes spread for 40 hors d'oeuvres.

Variation:
Substitute peanut butter for cream cheese.

Raisin Spread

Tonight, instead of raiding the refrigerator, try this economical spread.

1/4 cup chopped or whole raisins
1 cup finely ground, popped popcorn

Approximately 1 tablespoon sour cream or
  cottage cheese

Mix raisins and ground popcorn. Blend with enough sour cream or cottage cheese to make a spread. Spread on salty crackers. Makes spread for 16 crackers or filling for 2 sandwiches.

Sardine Spread Hors d'Oeuvres

Or use the spread to make delicious sandwiches.

1 cup finely ground, popped popcorn
1 (3-3/4-oz.) can sardines, drained
Salt and pepper to taste

3 to 5 tablespoons tomato sauce
Crackers or hot, buttered toast
1/2 cup grated cheese

Mix ground popcorn, sardines, salt and pepper with enough tomato sauce to make a paste. Spread on crackers or on hot, buttered toast. Sprinkle with grated cheese and serve at once. Makes spread for 30 crackers or filling for 4 sandwiches.

Variations:
Use catsup in place of tomato sauce.

Place under broiler just long enough to melt cheese.

Entrees

MAIN-DISH BUDGET STRETCHERS

What could be easier or more economical than measuring out a cup of ground popcorn, sprinkling in a few seasonings and using the mixture as a delicious coating mix for baked chicken or a crisp, flavorful crust for eggplant?

Today, when many of us are concerned about food additives and good nutrition, we talk about the good old days. We turn back to basic foods we know and trust, and rediscover popcorn. Popcorn is one of the oldest foods known to man. It can take its rightful place not only with traditional snacks, but with healthful ingredients used to cook a tasty, nutritious meal.

GROUND POPCORN

Many of the recipes in this section specify ground, popped popcorn. Grinding popcorn is very easy to do in a blender. It takes only a few minutes and you can grind enough popcorn at one time to store in a jar and use whenever a recipe calls for it.

Three different textures of ground popcorn are specified in this book—coarsely ground, medium-ground and finely ground.

Coarsely Ground Popcorn—Use your hands to lightly break apart the larger pieces of whole popcorn. About 1-1/2 cups of whole popcorn make 1 cup of coarsely ground popcorn.

Medium-Ground Popcorn—This can be made in a blender. Begin with a handful of whole popcorn. Turn the blender on Low for about 20 seconds or until all the popcorn has broken up. Empty into a bowl and repeat the procedure. About 1-1/2 cups of whole popcorn make 1 cup of medium-ground popcorn.

Finely Ground Popcorn—Place a handful of whole popcorn in the blender. Turn on Low for about a minute. The popcorn will flow like a thick syrup. Slowly add another handful or two of popcorn, letting the grinding continue for a minute or more. Empty the container and begin again. About 2 cups of whole popcorn make 1 cup of finely ground popcorn.

Popped popcorn can also be ground in a food processor.

Browned Cheese Mix

A terrific side dish.

2 cups coarsely ground, popped popcorn
2 cups water
1-1/2 cups grated cheese
1 cup coarsely ground, popped popcorn
6 tablespoons cornstarch

1/4 to 1/3 cup water
Grated onion to taste
Salt and pepper to taste
1 (8-oz.) can tomato sauce

Cook 2 cups ground popcorn in 2 cups of water for 30 minutes or until smooth. Preheat oven to 400°F (204°C). Butter a small baking pan. Remove popcorn from heat, add cheese and remaining 1 cup of popcorn. Dissolve cornstarch in 1/4 to 1/3 cup of water and add to popcorn mixture. Stir in onion, salt and pepper. Place in buttered baking pan. Bake for 20 to 30 minutes or until browned. Serve covered with warm tomato sauce. Makes 4 servings.

Clockwise from top right: Metal bowl of popped popcorn, glass jar of unpopped popcorn, medium-ground popcorn, finely ground popcorn, whole pieces of popped popcorn, coarsely ground popcorn.

Corny Chili Pie

The younger set really goes for this spicy, ranch-style, popcorn supper.

1 (10-oz.) can chili-hot-dog sauce
1 qt. popped popcorn
1 (10-oz.) pkg. corn-bread mix with
   plastic mixing bag
1 qt. popped popcorn

1 egg
1/2 cup milk
1 (8-oz.) can whole-kernel corn, drained;
   reserve 1 tablespoon liquid

Preheat oven to 425°F (218°C). Butter a 9" x 13" baking pan. Mix chili-hot-dog sauce and 1 quart of popcorn. Spread evenly in buttered baking pan. In the mixing bag, add and mix thoroughly the corn-bread mix, remaining 1 quart of popcorn, egg, milk, corn and the tablespoon of corn liquid. Place in a layer over chili-popcorn mixture. Bake for 20 minutes or until a cake tester can be removed clean from the center. Makes 6 servings.

Potato Casserole

A very easy and delicious luncheon dish.

2 cups hot mashed potatoes
   (3 or 4 medium-sized)
1 teaspoon finely chopped onion
1 tablespoon chopped fresh parsley

2 tablespoons butter
2-1/2 cups finely ground, popped popcorn
1 cup cottage cheese
1/2 cup grated cheddar cheese

Preheat oven to 350°F (177°C). Butter a 1-quart casserole. Mix together hot mashed potatoes, onion, parsley, butter, ground popcorn and cottage cheese. Spread in casserole. Sprinkle with cheddar cheese. Cover. Bake for 20 minutes. Makes 4 to 6 servings.

Beef-Rice Casserole

A quick and easy meal in one dish.

1 lb. ground beef
1/4 cup diced onion
1/4 cup diced celery
1 (10-3/4-oz.) can cream-of-chicken or
   cream-of-mushroom soup

1 can chicken-rice soup
4 cups finely ground, popped popcorn

Preheat oven to 350°F (177°C). In a skillet, brown ground beef, onion and celery. Combine with the remaining ingredients. Bake for 20 to 25 minutes. Makes 4 to 6 servings.

Stuffed Onions

A nifty vegetable treat.

2 tablespoons bread crumbs
5 tablespoons finely ground, popped popcorn
2 tablespoon butter
2 tablespoons chopped parsley

Salt and pepper to taste
Dash of paprika
1 egg, beaten
4 medium onions

Preheat oven to 350°F (177°C). In a small skillet, combine and cook bread crumbs, ground popcorn, butter, parsley, salt, pepper and paprika for 5 minutes. Remove from heat. Add egg and mix well. Remove the centers from onions and fill with the popcorn mixture. Bake for 1-1/4 hours. Makes 4 servings.

Fried Eggplant

Put this on the table with tossed salad, a cold beverage and, for dessert, fresh fruit and cheese.

1 eggplant
2 eggs, beaten
2 cups finely ground, popped popcorn

1 to 3 tablespoons bacon drippings or
    vegetable oil
Salt and pepper to taste

Wash eggplant. Pare if skin is tough. Cut crossways into 1/2-inch slices. Dip in egg, then in popcorn. In a large skillet, slowly brown on both sides in hot bacon drippings or vegetable oil. Add salt and pepper to taste. Makes 4 servings.

Hickory Meatloaf

Which secret ingredient is responsible for the slightly different flavor?

1-1/2 lbs. ground beef
1 small onion, chopped
1/3 cup milk
1 egg, beaten

3/4 cup hickory-flavored
    barbecue sauce,
6 cups finely ground, popped popcorn
Salt and pepper to taste

Preheat oven to 350°F (177°C). Mix ground beef, onion, milk, egg and barbecue sauce, reserving 2 tablespoons of sauce. Add ground popcorn, salt and pepper. Bake in a covered casserole or loaf pan for approximately 1 hour. Uncover the last 15 minutes and sprinkle with remaining 2 table-spoons of sauce. Makes 6 servings.

Stuffed Peppers

Something new has been added.

3 large green peppers
3 to 4 cups boiling, salted water
3/4 lb. ground beef
1 cup finely ground, popped popcorn
2 tablespoons finely chopped onions

1 teaspoon salt
1 teaspoon Worcestershire sauce
1/4 teaspoon pepper
1 (8-oz.) can tomato sauce

Preheat oven to 350°F (177°C). Cut peppers in half; remove seeds. Cook for 5 minutes in boiling, salted water. Drain. Mix other ingredients together and fill peppers. Bake in a covered casserole for 1 hour. Uncover and continue baking for 15 minutes. Makes 6 servings.

Pop 'N Bake Chicken

One editor claims this is the best chicken she ever ate!

1 (2-1/2 to 3-lb.) broiler-fryer chicken, cut up
1/2 to 1 cup finely ground, popped popcorn
2 teaspoons salt

1 teaspoon paprika
1/4 teaspoon pepper
1/4 cup vegetable oil

Preheat oven to 400°F (204°C). Wash chicken and pat dry. Mix together ground popcorn, salt, paprika and pepper. Coat chicken with popcorn mixture. Pour oil into shallow baking pan. Arrange chicken skin-side down in oil. Bake for 30 minutes. Turn chicken. Bake for 30 minutes more or until tender. Makes 4 servings.

Variations:
Add 1/4 teaspoon garlic powder and 1/2 teaspoon crushed tarragon to coating mix.

Measure seasonings and crushed herbs, if used, and mix into ground popcorn.

Roll chicken pieces in seasoned popcorn coating, lightly patting the coating onto the chicken if necessary.

Cornbread Stuffing

A subtle improvement on the traditional dish.

1/2 cup butter
1-1/2 cups chopped celery
1 cup minced onion
1/4 cup hot water
2 tablespoons minced parsley

1 teaspoon dried sage
2 (8-oz.) pkgs. cornbread-stuffing mix
1 cup finely ground, popped popcorn
1 (15 or 16-oz.) can cream-style corn

In a large skillet, melt butter. Sauté celery and onion in butter until transparent. Add water, parsley and sage, mixing well. Cook for 2 minutes. Mix in cornbread-stuffing mix and ground popcorn, blending thoroughly. Add corn and mix until moistened. Makes enough stuffing for a 14-pound turkey.

Variation:
Stuffing can be baked in a buttered casserole at 350°F (177°C) for about 30 minutes.

Stuffing Balls

Delicous as stuffing or a side dish.

2 cubes chicken bouillon
1/2 cup boiling water
1 (12-oz.) pkg. bulk sausage
1/2 cup butter, divided
1 cup thinly sliced celery
1 cup finely chopped onion

3 cups corn-bread-stuffing mix
8 cups finely ground, popped popcorn
1 teaspoon poultry seasoning
1 teaspoon parlsey flakes
Salt to taste
2 egg whites, beaten until foamy

Preheat oven to 325°F (163°C). Butter a large baking pan. Dissolve bouillon in boiling water. In a medium skillet, brown sausage and remove to a plate. Drain all but 1 tablespoon of fat from skillet. Loosen browned meat from the skillet with a spatula and add to sausage on plate. Melt 2 tablespoons butter in skillet. Add celery and onion. Cook, stirring until crisp-tender. Add remaining butter, stirring until melted. In a large mixing bowl combine stuffing mix and ground popcorn. Add browned sausage, poultry seasoning, parsley flakes, salt, celery mixture and bouillon mixture. Mix thoroughly. Add egg whites and mix again. Form into balls. Add a teaspoon of hot water if moisture is needed to hold shape. Place in buttered pan. Bake for 1 hour. Makes 10 stuffing balls.

Porkburgers

Sausage-popcorn patties stuffed with fruit and nuts!

1 lb. bulk pork sausage
1 egg, beaten
1/8 cup milk
1 teaspoon minced onion
1/4 teaspoon leaf sage
1/2 cup peeled, chopped apple

1/4 cup raisins
1/4 cup chopped nuts
1/4 teaspoon nutmeg
2 cups finely ground, popped popcorn
1/2 cup catsup, if desired

Preheat oven to 350°F (177°C). Mix together sausage, eggs, milk, onion and sage. Chill. Combine apple, raisins, nuts and nutmeg. Add ground popcorn to the sausage-egg mixture. Shape into 8 thin patties. Top 4 patties with 1/4 cup fruit mixture each. Top with remaining patties and seal the edges. Place on a rack in a shallow baking pan. Spread catsup on each patty, if desired. Bake about 45 minutes. Makes 4 servings.

Cornnut Loaf

You don't have to be a vegetarian to enjoy this meatless lunch.

1 cup finely ground, popped popcorn
1 cup soft bread crumbs
1 cup chopped nuts
1 teaspoon sage
Salt and pepper to taste

2 eggs, beaten
Approximately 2 tablespoons of
  cold water
1 (8-oz.) can tomato sauce

Preheat oven to 350°F (177°C). Butter a small baking pan. Mix ground popcorn, bread crumbs and nuts together. Mix in sage, salt and pepper. Add eggs and enough cold water to hold the mixture together. Form into a loaf and bake in the buttered pan for 45 minutes. Heat tomato sauce on medium heat. Cover loaf with warm tomato sauce and serve. Makes 2 servings.

DOES POPCORN HAVE A MASCOT?

Children may recognize the character in this clever drawing. His name is Whiskers and he has been immortalized in the children's book, *Whiskers the Bank Mouse.*

Whiskers lives in a bank and he loves spring. The reason he loves spring is because of popcorn! Springtime at Whiskers' bank means the arrival of a bright red and silver, antique popcorn wagon, and plenty to eat for Whiskers and his friends.

This story is based on fact. Every spring since 1910, an antique popcorn wagon has appeared alongside the Berkshire County Savings Bank in Pittsfield, Massachusetts. Every year the bank offers customers a new popcorn-related item, such as popcorn-wagon coin banks or decorative tiles.

On Thursdays, each bank customer receives a certificate for a free bag of popcorn from the popcorn wagon next door. And there are special Popcorn Savings Accounts for children. This has been so good for business, the bank has become known locally as "The Popcorn Bank."

Now "popcorn banks" are popping up all over the country. Ornate chrome and glass popcorn wagons stand outside banks in Illinois, Ohio, Pennsylvania and Mississippi. Some banks have small popcorn machines inside the bank. A familiar lunch-hour sight, even in sophisticated Chicago's banking district, is a long line of executives, secretaries, and clerks waiting for popcorn. It's reminiscent of the introduction of popcorn into movie theaters half a century ago.

Browned Nut Mix

If you don't tell, they'll probably think it's ground beef.

2 cups medium-ground, popped popcorn
2 cups water
4 tablespoons cornstarch
4 tablespoons water
2/3 cup finely chopped nuts

1 cup medium-ground, popped popcorn
2 eggs, beaten
Salt and pepper to taste
1 (10-oz.) can brown gravy

Cook 2 cups ground popcorn in 2 cups water for 30 minutes or until smooth. Preheat oven to 350°F (177°C). Butter a small baking pan. Dissolve cornstarch in 4 tablespoons water. Combine popcorn-water mixture, nuts, remaining 1 cup of ground popcorn, eggs, cornstarch-water mixture, salt, pepper and half of gravy. Mix well. If necessary, add just enough water to shape into a loaf. Place in buttered pan. Bake for 20 minutes or until browned. Serve covered with remaining warmed gravy. Makes 4 servings.

Popcorn Patties

Delicious served hot and covered with tomato sauce.

2 cups bread crumbs
2 cups medium-ground, popped popcorn
1 cup cream or milk
2 eggs
Salt and pepper to taste

6 tablespoons flour
2 to 3 tablespoons butter
1 (8-oz.) can tomato sauce
Fresh chopped parsley

In a large bowl, mix bread crumbs, ground popcorn, cream or milk, eggs, salt and pepper thoroughly. Mold into patties. Coat with flour. In a large skillet, melt butter. Add patties and brown on both sides. Heat tomato sauce on medium heat. Garnish patties with parsley and warm tomato sauce. Makes 6 patties.

Popcorn Roast

As satisfying as the real thing. Enjoy it with your favorite sauce or gravy.

2 cups bread crumbs
1/2 cup chopped nuts
1/2 cup medium-ground, popped popcorn
1/2 cup hot water
1/2 cup melted butter

1/2 teaspoon instant minced onion
1-1/2 teaspoon salt
1/4 teaspoon pepper
1 egg, beaten
1/4 cup or less melted butter

Preheat oven to 350°F (177°C). Butter a small mold or loaf pan. Thoroughly mix all ingredients except 1/4 cup melted butter. Place in buttered mold or loaf pan and bake for 1 hour. Cover the first 15 minutes, then baste 3 times with 1/4 cup or less melted butter. Turn out into a hot dish and serve with your favorite sauce or gravy. Makes 4 servings.

Macaroni

Rich and creamy with unexpected flavor.

2 cups uncooked macaroni
Water
1/2 cup butter
1/2 cup flour
Salt to taste

Pepper to taste
2 cups milk
4 cups finely ground, popped popcorn
1 cup buttered bread crumbs
1/2 cup grated cheese

Preheat oven to 400°F (204°C). Butter a medium-sized baking dish. Cook macaroni in water according to package directions. Drain and pour cold water through to separate the pieces. In a medium saucepan, melt butter over low heat. Stir in flour, salt and pepper. Remove from heat. Slowly add milk, stirring constantly, until smooth. Return to low heat. Stir constantly until sauce thickens. Add to macaroni. Stir in ground popcorn and mix well. Pour into buttered baking dish. Top with bread crumbs and grated cheese. Bake 20 to 30 minutes or until golden brown. Makes 6 servings.

Breads

MADE WITH NUTRITIOUS POPCORN FLOUR

After World War II, wheat, rye and other grains were in short supply. The search began for a substitute flour to be used in bread. The answer was popcorn flour, ground from kernels unfit for popping because of frostbite or other reasons. After some experimentation, a loaf consisting of 75% wheat flour and 25% popcorn flour was sold successfully. Muffins and doughnuts made with popcorn flour could also be bought. Products with popcorn flour disappeared as soon as the other grains became available again. Now you can bake your own popcorn-flour bread with the recipes in this section.

GROUND POPCORN

To make popcorn flour for the bread recipes in this section, grind popped popcorn in your blender. Put a handful of popped popcorn in the blender. Turn the blender on Low. For medium-ground popcorn, leave the blender on for about 20 seconds or until all the popcorn has broken up. For finely ground popcorn, leave the blender on for about a minute. Empty the ground popcorn into a jar or canister and put another handful or so in the blender. Grind several cupfuls and store in a tightly covered canister or jar so you'll always have ground popcorn on hand when a recipe calls for it.

Popped popcorn can also be ground in a food processor.

FRESH OR HOT?

Many people confuse hot popcorn with fresh popcorn and cold popcorn with stale popcorn. Theaters have found that if popcorn is freshly popped, but allowed to cool, more complaints are made than if the popcorn is older, but hot.

Honey Buns

Very easy. Very good.

8 teaspoons honey
1 cup finely ground, popped popcorn
1 (12 oz.) pkg. refrigerated
   dinner-roll dough

1 teaspoon cinnamon
1/4 cup halved maraschino cherries

Preheat oven to 350°F (177°C). Butter an 8-cup muffin tin. Mix honey and ground popcorn. Divide mixture evenly in muffin cups. Unwrap dinner-roll dough. Spread out and sprinkle with cinnamon. Fold edges of each roll over cinnamon, forming bun shapes. Place seam sides down over popcorn and honey in muffin cups. Bake for 20 minutes or until tops are brown. Place buns upside down on serving dish. Garnish with cherries. Serve hot. Makes 8 muffins.

Pocket Bread

This bread puffs up to form a pocket to hold your sandwich filling.

2 envelopes dry yeast
2-1/2 cups warm water
1 tablespoon sugar
1 tablespoon salt

1 tablespoon vegetable oil
2 cups finely ground, popped popcorn,
   divided into 2 cups
5 cups flour

Sprinkle yeast over water in a large bowl and stir until dissolved. Stir in sugar, salt, oil, 1 cup ground popcorn and enough flour to make a sticky dough. Turn out onto a well-floured board and knead until smooth and elastic, about 10 minutes, working in remaining flour and popcorn as needed. Shape dough into 12-inch roll. Cut into 12 pieces. Knead each piece until smooth and round. Roll out each ball into a circle 1/8-inch thick. Place on a well-floured surface and cover with a cloth. Let stand for 2 hours or until dough has risen slightly. Preheat oven to 450°F (232°C). Turn each bread over and place on ungreased cooky sheets, 3 breads to a sheet. Bake 2 pans at a time for 5 minutes or until bread puffs up. Place under the broiler for 2 minutes or until lightly browned. Remove from oven. Cover with towel until cooled. Repeat with remaining bread. Makes 12 individual pocket breads.

Cottage-Cheese Bread

Try this bread for breakfast with a cup of steaming hot chocolate.

1/2 cup butter
1/2 cup sugar
2 eggs
1 tablespoon grated lemon peel
1 pt. creamed small-curd cottage cheese
1/3 cup chopped dates, raisins or
   other dried fruit

1/2 teaspoon salt
1/2 teaspoon baking soda
2 teaspoons baking powder
2 cups flour
2 cups finely ground, popped popcorn
Powdered sugar

Preheat oven to 350°F (177°C). Butter a 9-inch ring mold. Thoroughly mix butter and sugar. Beat in eggs, lemon peel, and cottage cheese. Mix dried fruit, salt, baking soda, baking powder, flour and ground popcorn. Combine with cottage-cheese mixture and spoon into ring mold. Bake 40 minutes or until pick inserted in center comes out dry. Cool 10 minutes, then invert on wire rack to continue cooling. Dust with powdered sugar. Makes 1 loaf ring.

Variation:
To make a colorful Christmas bread, add 1/4 cup candied cherries and 1/4 cup diced candied pine-apple with the dried fruit.

Granola Muffins

Hot muffins with a nutty, apple flavor.

1/2 cup medium-ground, popped popcorn
1/2 cup granola
1-1/4 cups unsifted all-purpose flour
1/2 cup brown sugar, firmly packed
2 teaspoons baking powder
1 teaspoon salt
1 teaspoon cinnamon

1/4 teaspoon baking soda
1 tablespoon lemon juice
1 cup milk
1 egg, beaten
1/3 cup butter, melted
1/2 cup finely chopped red apples

Preheat oven to 400°F (204°C). Butter two 8-cup muffin tins or line with paper liners. In a large mixing bowl, combine dry ingredients. Add lemon juice to milk and mix with egg, melted butter and chopped apple. Add to dry ingredients, stirring until well moistened. Fill each muffin cup about 2/3 full. Bake about 25 minutes. Makes 16 muffins.

NUTRITION

Popcorn is one of the few snack foods that both tastes good and is good for you. It is one of the best all-around snacks in existence.

Popcorn is a whole grain. Its nutritive values are retained inside the hull until it is popped. The U.S. Department of Agriculture has found the following nutritive values in 1 pint of popped popcorn. The figures vary because the actual weight of a pint of popcorn depends on the size of the pieces. They found a pint weighed from 1/2 to 1 ounce (12 to 28 grams) and contained 50 to 110 calories. Carbohydrates accounted for 10 to 22 grams of that weight, protein from 2 to 4 grams and fat from 1 to 2 grams. One pint of popcorn contained 2 milligrams of calcium, 0.4 to 0.6 milligrams of iron, 0.2 to 0.6 milligrams of niacin, .02 milligrams of riboflavin and traces of vitamin A and thiamin. Water made up about 4% of the total weight.

These figures may not seem very high, but compared ounce for ounce with beef, popcorn provides 67% as much protein, 110% as much iron, and an equal amount of calcium. A pint of popcorn contains 3 times as much phosphorus as a pint of milk. An average serving of 1-1/2 ounces of popcorn supplies as much energy as two eggs. A cup of unbuttered popcorn contains less calories than half a medium grapefruit.

YOUR TEETH AND POPCORN

The American Dental Association recommends popcorn as a snack because it's sugar-free. Chewing popped popcorn also helps your teeth and gums because it has a mild cleansing and massaging effect.

POPCORN FOR DIETING

Popcorn is ideal for between-meal nibbling. Eaten immediately before a meal it will take the edge off your appetite with just a few calories. Many diets include popcorn as a substitute for bread. The cellulose of the hull is an indigestable carbohydrate, an excellent roughage which compares favorably with bran flakes or whole-wheat toast. Digestible carbohydrates also contained in popcorn provide energy and help the body metabolize fats.

If you are dieting, you don't have to give up popcorn. It's the butter on the popcorn that's fattening. Lightly salted popcorn is delicious without butter—and a lot lower in calories.

Camp-Out Popcorn

Measure oil and unpopped popcorn into the foil square. Bring corners and edges of foil together. Twist to close.

Fasten foil packet with string or wire to end of stick. Hold over fire and shake when popcorn begins to pop.

Hobo Popcorn

Make it over the campfire in an aluminum-foil pouch.

4 tablespoons oil
4 tablespoons unpopped popcorn
4 (12-in.-square) pieces heavy-duty
   aluminum foil

4 tablespoons melted butter
Salt to taste

Place 1 tablespoon of oil and 1 tablespoon of unpopped popcorn in the center of each foil square. Twist the ends together to make a pouch. Tightly attach to a stick with wire or string and place over hot coals or a grill. As soon as popcorn begins to pop, start shaking the pouch over the fire. When the popping stops, open carefully because the pouch may be full of hot steam. Pour melted butter over the popcorn, and eat it right from the pouch. Makes 4 servings.

Popcorn Pack-Eats

Make your own dessert around the campfire.

2 qts. unsalted popped popcorn
4 large squares of heavy-duty aluminum foil
1/2 to 1 cup semi-sweet chocolate or
  butterscotch cooking chips

1/2 to 1 cup miniature marshmallows
1/2 to 1 cup salted pecans or peanuts

Let each person place 2 cups of popped popcorn in the center of a foil square and top with candy and nuts. Bring the corners of the foil up over the popcorn and fold or pinch the top and ends to make a closed packet. Place the packet on a grill over ashen-gray coals or in a 350° F (177°C) oven until well heated, about 10 minutes. Turn once if well-sealed. Remove from heat. Open packet, being careful to avoid any escaping steam. Makes 4 packets.

Back-Packer's Mix

Something for the summit.

2 qts. popped popcorn
1 cup salted or unsalted peanuts
1 cup raisins

1 cup shredded fresh coconut
1 cup sunflower seeds
Salt, if desired

Make sure the popcorn is cool. Mix well with all ingredients. Pack loosely in foil-lined bags, clean, dry milk cartons, converted coffee cans with plastic covers or in plastic sandwich bags. Makes approximately 3 quarts.

CAMP-OUT POPCORN

Popcorn kernels are small, light and easy to carry in a backpack. They are delicious when popped in a covered skillet over a hot bed of coals. If you don't have a cover for the skillet, use aluminum foil. Puncture the foil in 2 or 3 places to make a vent for the steam. Drippings from bacon, sausage or hamburger make a flavorful popping oil. Be careful not to burn your hands.

One trick to make cleaning the pan easier is to scrape the outside surface with hand soap before you use it. This protects it from the soot, at least partly. Another trick is to use an aluminum pouch. Either way, you get a great snack.

A little of the popcorn may burn and some may not pop, but on a camping trip you'll think it's the best in the world. Don't forget to take along your popcorn salt.

THE CURDS AND WHY
OF THEATER POPCORN

A common frustration among popcorn lovers is their failure to duplicate the special flavor of popcorn sold in theaters. Even when they imitate the pros and use coconut oil and popcorn-seasoning salt, their popcorn still tastes different.

Some have concluded that the difference is in the surroundings. Popcorn tastes better because theaters have a special "feel." Others have concocted elaborate mixtures of herbs and spices hoping to duplicate that special flavor—and they have failed.

The secret is not in the surroundings. The secret is not an elaborate mix. The solution to this mystery lies in what the pros pour over their popcorn—the butter.

Regular butter, the kind you find in the grocery store, is not used in theaters because it contains curd. Curd is a solid that separates from the butter when it's heated and forms a solid layer on top. It clogs butter dispensers. Instead of regular butter, pros use *anhydrous* butter—butter from which the curds and whey have been removed. Whey is water, which solves another long-standing mystery concerning Miss Muffet.

Anhydrous butter is a concentrate made of almost pure butterfat. Its flavor and odor are similar to fresh, unsalted creamery butter. This makes the flavor of the popcorn and the seasoning salt stand out. But flavor is not the only reason for using anhydrous butter. The butter must melt properly.

Anhydrous butter melts at room temperature. It melts in your mouth. Your body temperature makes it melt even after the popcorn has cooled and the butter has solidified. Butter that only melts when heated above body temperature remains a solid in your mouth and leaves a waxy aftertaste.

Some butter-flavored oils are also used by the pro's. These oils usually consist of 97% or more coconut or vegetable oil plus some anhydrous butterfat, butter oil, artificial flavor and color. Butter-flavored oils may be used alone or mixed with anhydrous butterfat.

Popcorn Candy

HOW CRACKER JACK® GOT ITS NAME

A big hit at the 1893 Chicago World's Fair was a molasses-coated popcorn and peanut confection scooped out of a barrel.

The creator of this confection, F.W. Rueckheim, a German immigrant, hadn't given his product a name. The story varies, but in 1896 a salesman tasted the molasses-popcorn-peanut delicacy, smacked his lips and announced, "Now that's a crackerjack!" The name stuck. Later that year, Cracker Jack® appeared packaged in individual boxes that sold for a nickel. This price didn't change for more than half a century. In 1912, people began finding prizes in their Cracker Jack® packages, a tradition now considered as American as apple pie and, well, popcorn.

Preparing good popcorn candy is not all luck. If you are not sure of exactly how much of an ingredient to mix into your syrup, add the ingredient slowly and taste-test the mixture several times. The flavor won't change when the syrup is mixed with the popcorn. It's easy to add more of an ingredient if it's needed, but impossible to remove if you have added too much.

Popcorn Divinity

Sweet and chewy with a spicy surprise.

2 qts. popped popcorn
1/4 cup light corn syrup
1 cup sugar
1/2 cup water

10 marshmallows
1 teaspoon almond extract
2-1/2 tablespoons cinnamon drops

Preheat oven to 250°F (121°C). Place popcorn in a large, 4-inch-deep, buttered baking pan. Keep warm in the oven. Butter a 9-inch-square baking pan. Mix together corn syrup, sugar and water in a large saucepan. Cook over medium heat, stirring constantly, until mixture boils. Cook without stirring until mixture reaches 240°F (116°C) on a candy thermometer. Remove from heat. Quickly add marshmallows and almond extract, stirring until marshmallows melt and blend with syrup. Stir in cinnamon drops. Remove popcorn from oven. Pour syrup over popcorn and toss until well coated. Press mixture into buttered baking pan. Press any remaining mixture into small buttered custard cups. Let stand until cool and firm. Cut into squares. Makes 16 squares.

Variation:
To make Christmas Divinity, use green candy drops for half the cinnamon drops.

Maple-Coated Corn

Fill a large canister, top with a brightly colored bow, and give as a gift.

2 tablespoons butter
3/4 cup maple syrup

1/2 cup sugar
1-1/2 qts. popped popcorn

Preheat oven to 250°F (121°C). Place popcorn in a large, 4-inch-deep, buttered baking pan. Keep warm in the oven. Cut a large sheet of wax paper to fit a cooky sheet. Lightly butter the wax paper. Cook butter, maple syrup, and sugar until mixture reaches 275°F (135°C) on a candy thermometer. Remove popcorn from oven. Pour syrup mixture over popcorn, stirring constantly. Spread hot, coated popcorn on wax paper until cool. Break into pieces and store in a covered container. Makes 1-1/2 quarts.

Chocolate Squares

Popcorn, chocolate and marshmallow—a super combination!

1 (7-oz.) jar marshmallow creme
1 cup semi-sweet chocolate cooking chips

1/4 cup light corn syrup
1-1/2 qts. popped popcorn

Preheat oven to 250°F (121°C). Place popcorn in a large, 4-inch-deep, buttered baking pan. Keep warm in the oven. Butter a 9-inch-square baking pan. Combine marshmallow creme, chocolate cooking chips and corn syrup in a saucepan. Cook over low heat until well blended. Remove popcorn from oven. Pour syrup mixture over popcorn. Mix well. Press into the buttered baking pan. Cut into large squares. Makes 16 squares.

Becky's Chocolate-Covered Popcorn

A tasty delight, well worth the time.

1 cup milk chocolate
2 tablespoons sugar

1 cup popped popcorn

Lightly butter a large plate. Warm chocolate and sugar over very low heat. Spread popped popcorn on a buttered plate, well separated. Using a teaspoon, cover each piece of popcorn with a small amount of the chocolate. Place in the freezer at least 15 minutes before serving. Makes about 40 pieces.

Peanutty Chocolate Bars

This blend of chocolate and peanut butter is always a winner.

1/2 cup butter
1 cup light-brown sugar, firmly packed
1/4 cup light corn syrup
1/4 cup water
1 teaspoon salt

2 qts. popped popcorn
1 heaping cup milk-chocolate cooking chips
1 cup chunky peanut butter
Peanuts for garnish

Preheat oven to 250°F (121°C). Place popcorn in a large, 4-inch-deep, buttered baking pan. Keep warm in the oven. Butter a 15-1/2" x 10-1/2" x 1" baking pan. Melt butter in a large saucepan. Stir in brown sugar, corn syrup, water and salt. Cook over medium heat, stirring constantly, until sugar is dissolved and mixture begins to boil. Continue cooking until mixture reaches 250°F (121°C) on a candy thermometer. Remove popcorn from oven. Pour caramel mixture slowly over popcorn, stirring to coat. Press caramel-coated popcorn into buttered baking pan. In a saucepan, heat chocolate cooking chips and peanut butter together over low heat, stirring constantly, until chocolate is melted. Spread evenly over caramel popcorn. Cool until chocolate-peanut-butter topping is set. Cut onto 2" x 2" bars and garnish with whole peanuts. Makes approximately 40 bars.

Popcorn-Peanut Clusters

Something to please the President.

1/3 cup sugar
3 tablespoons molasses
3 tablespoons dark corn syrup
1 teaspoon butter

1 teaspoon lemon juice
1 (6-1/2-oz.) can peanuts
1 qt. popped popcorn

Cut a large piece of wax paper to fit a cooky sheet. Lightly butter the wax paper. Combine sugar, molasses, corn syrup, butter and lemon juice in a large saucepan. Heat slowly, stirring constantly, until sugar is dissolved. Remove from heat. Stir the peanuts and popcorn into mixture until evenly coated. Return to heat and cook, stirring continuously, for 5 minutes. Mixture should be sticky. Spread out on buttered wax paper. Cool until easy to handle, then shape into bite-size clusters. Wrap individually and store in a loosely covered container. Makes approximately 1-1/4 quarts.

Candied Fruit Squares

These will brighten your day.

2 qts. popped popcorn
1 cup sugar

1/3 cup dark or light corn syrup
1/2 cup chopped, mixed candied fruits

Preheat oven to 250°F (121°C). Place popcorn in a large, 4-inch-deep, buttered baking pan. Keep warm in the oven. Butter a 9-inch-square glass baking dish. In a large saucepan, cook sugar and corn syrup until mixture reaches 250°F (121°C) on a candy thermometer. Remove from heat and add finely chopped candied fruits. Remove popcorn from oven. Pour syrup mixture immediately over popcorn and stir until well mixed. Pack into buttered baking dish. When hardened, cut into squares. Makes 36 squares.

Variation:
Substitute spiced gum drops for candied fruit.

Popcorn Brittle

Good 'n crunchy.

1 cup butter
1 cup sugar
2 tablespoons water

1 tablespoon light corn syrup
1 qt. popped popcorn
1/2 cup granola

Cut a large sheet of wax paper to fit a cooky sheet. Lightly butter the wax paper. Melt butter in a 3-quart saucepan over low heat. Remove from heat and blend in sugar. Return to low heat, stirring constantly, until mixture reaches a full boil. Stir in water and corn syrup. Continue stirring over low heat until mixture reaches 270°F (132°C) on a candy thermometer. Remove from heat. Stir in popcorn and granola. Cool until hardened. Break into large pieces. Makes approximately one quart.

Variation:
Mix chopped nuts with cereal before sprinkling.

Chocolate Fudge

Take some to a friend.

2 cups sugar
1 cup milk
2 squares semi-sweet cooking chocolate
1 tablespoon butter

1/4 teaspoon salt
1 teaspoon vanilla
1 cup coarsely ground, popped popcorn

Butter an 8-inch-square baking pan. Combine sugar, milk, chocolate squares, butter and salt. Cook until mixture reaches 235°F (113°C) on a candy thermometer. Remove from heat. Add vanilla and ground popcorn. Stir until mixture is creamy but still soft. Pour into buttered baking pan. Cut into squares when cool. Makes 16 squares.

Peanut-Butter Fudge

A rich, easy-to-make fudge for peanut-butter lovers.

1/2 cup peanut butter
1/2 cup milk
2-1/2 cups sugar

1 teaspoon butter
1-1/2 cups coarsely ground, popped popcorn
1 teaspoon vanilla

Butter an 8-inch-square pan. In a large saucepan, mix together peanut butter, milk and sugar. Cook until mixture reaches 235°F (118°C) on a candy thermometer. Quickly add butter, ground popcorn and vanilla. Beat until creamy. Pour into pan to cool. Cut into squares. Makes 36 squares.

Molasses Candy

Old-fashioned ingredients in a new combination.

2 cups molasses
1 cup brown sugar, firmly packed
1 tablespoon butter
1 tablespoon vinegar

Large pinch of salt
2 cups popped popcorn
1/2 teaspoon almond extract

Butter an 8-inch-square baking pan. In a large saucepan, boil molasses, brown sugar, butter and vinegar until mixture reaches 300°F (149°C) on a candy thermometer. Just before removing from heat, stir in a large pinch of salt, popcorn and almond extract. Pour into buttered pan. Cut into squares before it cools. Makes 16 squares.

St. Patrick's Day Popcorn

A little eatin' o' the green.

3 qts. popped popcorn
1/2 cup butter
1 cup sugar
1/2 teaspoon salt

1/4 cup light corn syrup
1/2 teaspoon peppermint extract
1/8 teaspoon green food coloring

Preheat oven to 250°F (121°C). Place the popcorn in a large, 4-inch-deep, buttered baking pan. Keep warm in the oven. Butter a 15-1/2" x 10-1/2" x 1" pan. In a large saucepan, melt butter over low heat. Stir in sugar, salt and corn syrup. Cook, stirring constantly, until sugar dissolves and mixture comes to a boil. Boil, without stirring, for 5 minutes. Remove from heat. Stir in peppermint extract and green food coloring. Remove popcorn from oven. Pour syrup mixture over popcorn and stir to mix well. Spread on buttered pan. Bake for 1 hour, stirring 3 or 4 times. Cool completely. Break or cut into pieces. Store in a tightly covered container. Makes 3 quarts.

Rocky-Road Fudge

Place the marshmallows in the freezer the night before.

6 large marshmallows cut in quarters or
   24 miniature marshmallows
6 squares semi-sweet cooking chocolate
1/2 cup butter
2 cups sugar

10 large, whole marshmallows
2/3 cup evaporated milk
1/2 cup chopped walnuts
1 cup coarsely ground, popped popcorn
1 teaspoon vanilla

Place quartered or miniature marshmallows on a tray or cooky sheet. Freeze until firm. Lightly butter an 8-inch-square pan. Place chocolate squares and butter in a large bowl and set aside. Combine sugar, whole marshmallows and evaporated milk in a large saucepan. Bring to a boil over medium heat and continue boiling for 5 minutes, stirring constantly. Pour over chocolate squares and butter. Stir until mixture is well blended and begins to thicken. Add walnuts, ground popcorn, vanilla and frozen marshmallows. Pour into buttered pan. Chill until firm. Cut into squares. Store, covered, in a cool place. Makes approximately 24 pieces.

Hint:
Use scissors to cut marshmallows.

Marshmallow Balls

Delight the young crowd by serving these on lollypop sticks.

1 (1-lb). pkg. marshmallows
1/4 cup butter

3 qts. popped popcorn
3 (3 to 4-in.) hard-candy sticks, crushed

Heat marshmallows and butter in top of double boiler or over low heat until melted and smooth. Pour over popcorn and mix well. Let stand several minutes before forming into balls or bars. Roll in crushed candy. Makes 12 balls.

Caramel Corn

Good munching.

2 qts. popped popcorn
1 (1-lb.) bag caramels

1/4 cup water
1 cup peanuts

Preheat oven to 250°F (121°). Place popcorn in a large 4-inch deep, buttered baking pan. Keep warm in the oven. Place caramels and water in top of double boiler. Heat over boiling water, stirring frequently, until caramels are melted. Add peanuts and mix well. Remove popcorn from oven. Pour syrup slowly over popcorn, tossing to coat well. Let stand until firm, break apart to serve. Makes 3 quarts.

Andy's Candy

Simple to make.

1 cup brown sugar, firmly packed
1 cup molasses

1/2 cup butter
2 cups finely ground, popped popcorn

Butter an 8-inch-square baking pan. Cook brown sugar, molasses, and butter in a medium saucepan until mixture reaches 250°F (121°C) on a candy thermometer. Add ground popcorn and mix well. Pour into buttered pan. When partially cool, cut into squares. Cut again when completely cool. Makes 16 squares.

Gum-Drop Squares

Make these during the holidays and add a few more gum drops.

1 (1-lb.) pkg. marshmallows
1/3 cup butter
1 teaspoon vanilla

1 cup spiced gum drops
3 qts. popped popcorn

Butter a 9" x 13" glass baking dish. Place marshmallows and butter in top of double boiler. Heat over hot water until smooth. Blend in vanilla and gum drops. Pour over popcorn and mix to coat well. Press into buttered baking dish. Cut when cool, then again when cold. Cover with plastic wrap and store in refrigerator. Makes 28 squares.

Variation:
Use nuts or shredded coconut in place of gum drops.

GROW YOUR OWN

Why not grow your own popcorn this summer? Many varieties of seeds can be obtained from any good nursery, seed store or seed catalog. Check to see which type will grow best in your area.

Plant in a sunny location. A rich, sandy loam that drains well will give the best results. Popcorn requires a lot of nitrogen and grows well in soil with a high organic-matter content. If you think your soil isn't rich enough, don't hesitate to fertilize.

Plant in May or early June. Popcorn takes about 100 days to mature. If you are also growing sweet corn, plant the popcorn well away to avoid cross-pollination. The cross will make your popcorn pop poorly and make your sweet corn hard.

Plant the seeds according to package directions. Usually this will be in rows or hills 2 to 3-feet apart. Three or four rows 4 or 5-feet long should produce more than enough popcorn to last a season. It is better to plant several short rows than a few long ones if only a small amount is to be grown.

The plants should be set 12 to 15-inches apart in the rows, or 3 plants per hill. Plant closely and thin out the weak plants. Do not allow the plants to grow too close together because they can inhibit each other's growth.

Keep the patch free of weeds, especially when the popcorn plants are small. Water often and occasionally break up the soil with a hoe so air and water can circulate freely. In hot climates, a mulch of grass clippings will reduce the amount of water needed.

POPPING QUALITY

Popping quality depends on the maturity of the ears when they are removed from the stalk. The longer they cure in the field, the better the popcorn will be. The two chief dangers are birds and frost. Either can ruin your crop, and the only solution may be to harvest. The husks should be completely white, and the kernels very hard before the ears are picked. The kernels should not seep milk when cut. If your thumbnail can puncture the kernel, the corn isn't ready.

Pick the ears when ready, strip off the husks, and store the popcorn ears where they can dry for several months. Popcorn pops best when the moisture level is between 13% and 14.5%, but it may be as high as 20% when harvested. It is best to dry the ears naturally by the circulation of air. Artificial heat or forced air may ruin their taste. Hang the ears or spread them on a table. Turn them occasionally so they will dry evenly and not mold. It may be December or January before the popcorn is ready for use.

Test your popcorn by picking a few kernels and popping them. When they pop properly, remove all kernels from the cobs and store them in airtight containers in a cool place.

Sculptures & Shapes

The difference between a popcorn shape and a popcorn sculpture is the size and complexity of the object being made.

Popcorn shapes are usually smaller than sculptures and are made primarily for fun eating. Many different and tasty recipes can be made into shapes. Look in the section on Balls, Bars and Crunches, pages 56 to 80, for a recipe that appeals to you.

Popcorn sculptures are made to be admired. They can be 1-foot tall or 10-feet tall. Some sculptures have been as large as 20-feet tall and weighed over 1000 pounds. Sculptures are usually made with plain syrup and sugar recipe and often contain a lot of food coloring, see page 131.

All you need is a little imagination. If you can't think of anything to make at first, here are a few ideas. Once you get started, you'll find you have more creative ideas than you realized.

Shapes and sculptures make special occasions into particularly memorable events. Make bunnies or eggs for Easter, jack-o-lanterns for Halloween, snowmen and trees for Christmas and ornaments for the Christmas tree. You can make a popcorn shape or sculpture on almost any theme.

Make a cat with whiskers of colored toothpicks and a black jelly bean for a nose.

Children will love popcorn teddy bears. Make a large popcorn ball for the body and smaller shapes for the head, arms, and legs. Attach them with toothpicks. Use gumdrops and other candy or raisins for the nose, ears, eyes and buttons.

To make a snowman, stack popcorn balls on top of each other. Secure them with skewers, if necessary. Use candy and raisins for eyes, nose and buttons and a licorice strip for his mouth. Place a doll's hat on his head.

To make miniature Christmas trees, lightly pack popcorn coated with green syrup into wax-paper cones. Or gently stack syrup-coated popcorn around an upside-down flower pot. Or mold the popcorn mixture over a styrofoam cone, attaching it at intervals with toothpicks. Decorate your tree with gumdrops, tiny candy canes and silver cake decorations.

Once you decide what you want to make, get someone to help. Making popcorn shapes and sculptures is an exciting and creative family activity. Everyone from toddlers to grandparents will enjoy shaping, arranging and decorating. You can all work on one large sculpture or each person can create an individual shape.

Use your imagination to find molds to make the various shapes. Shape very large balls, one half at a time, in buttered mixing bowls. Stick the halves together to make 1 large ball. Make cylindrical shapes by packing popcorn inside buttered cans with the tops and bottoms removed.

You'll soon discover a variety of materials right in your own kitchen, desk or sewing basket. Some of the most common items you might use are pipe cleaners, colored straws, ribbons, doilies, paper coasters, crepe paper, toothpicks and scraps of sewing materials.

Mold syrup-coated popcorn into desired shapes. Press shapes together. If necessary, use toothpicks to attach one shape to another.

Use small pieces of candy to make faces and other details. Press the candy on while the syrup is still wet so the candy will stick. Attach marshmallows with toothpicks.

A FEW HINTS

1. Work fast. The popcorn-syrup mixture hardens while you're working with it.

2. Make the syrup in small amounts so it won't harden before you can use it all.

3. To reduce the amount of popcorn and syrup required, build large shapes or sculptures around cans or small boxes.

4. Wear rubber gloves. Keep them lightly buttered or wet them occasionally with water.

POPCORN PICTURES

On a rainy afternoon at home, children enjoy making popcorn pictures. Pieces of popcorn pasted onto brightly colored construction paper, make excellent snowflakes, bears, clouds, snow-covered trees and other intriguing shapes. Give children popcorn kernels, raisins, buttons and other small items they can use in making their popcorn pictures.

The world's leading popcorn sculptors can be found at the Karmelkorn® Shoppes, a national chain of stores specializing in such popcorn products as caramel corn, popcorn, cheese corn and popcorn balls.

Sculptures similar to these are made and sold at Karmelkorn® Shoppes.

Harvest Pumpkin Ball

Cinderella's pumpkin turns into a dessert.

4 qts. popped popcorn
1/4 cups water
1 teaspoon pumpkin-pie spice
1/4 teaspoon salt

1 lb. vanilla caramels
35 to 40 in. shoestring licorice
4 to 6 green gumdrops

Place popcorn in a large bowl. Combine water, pumpkin-pie spice and salt in the top of a double boiler. Mix well. Add caramels and cook over hot water, stirring often, until caramels are melted and mixture is smooth. Pour over popcorn. Toss until the pieces are well coated. With lightly buttered hands, form into a pumpkin shape measuring about 8 inches in diameter at the bottom and about 4-1/2 inches high at the center. Make 7 or 8 slight indentations from the center to the bottom to form sections of the pumpkin. Cut strips of shoestring licorice and press down the center of each indentation. Use green gumdrops to make a pumpkin stem. Use as a centerpiece for the table. If desired, arrange with a cornucopia of fresh red and green apples, grapes and nuts. Makes 1 large ball.

Tasty Syrup-Coated Popcorn For Shapes & Sculptures

Fun to make and delicious, too.

2 qts. unbuttered popped popcorn
1 cup sugar
1/3 cup light corn syrup
1/3 cup water

4 tablespoons butter
1/2 teaspoon salt
1 teaspoon vanilla
Food coloring, if desired

Preheat oven to 250°F (121°C). Place popcorn in a large, 4-inch-deep, buttered baking pan and keep warm in oven. In a large saucepan, mix sugar, corn syrup, water, butter and salt. Cook over medium heat, stirring constantly, until mixture comes to a boil. Continue cooking until mixture reaches 265°F (129°C) on a candy thermometer. Remove from heat. Quickly stir in the vanilla. If desired, add food coloring. Remove popcorn from oven. Pour syrup over popcorn. Stir with a large spoon just until the syrup is evenly distributed. Make the desired shapes or sculptures. Makes 2 quarts of syrup-coated popcorn.

Popcorn Wreath

Santa's elves were here.

4 qts. popped popcorn
1 batch of Light-Syrup Glaze, see page 142
Green food coloring
1 foot of heavy string or wire

1/2 to 1 cup cinnamon drops,
   silver cake-decorating candy or both
Ribbons or other decorations, if desired

Preheat oven to 250°F (121°C). Place popcorn in a large, 4-inch-deep, buttered baking pan. Keep warm in the oven. On a large, flat pan or surface, draw 2 concentric circles with pencil: the inside circle 7 inches in diameter, and the outside one 14 inches in diameter. Butter the pan between the 2 lines, taking care not to erase the lines. Add enough food coloring, a drop at a time, to the glaze to make a dark green. Remove popcorn from oven. If you glaze half the popcorn at a time, be careful that the glaze remaining in the pan doesn't burn while you're mixing the first half. Pour glaze over the popcorn. Mix well. Pile the popcorn-glaze mixture between the lines drawn on the pan or surface, forming into a wreath shape between the 2 lines. Insert half of the string or wire into the still-pliable mixture. This will be used to hang the finished wreath. Sprinkle the wreath with cinnamon drops, silver candy or both. If desired, attach bells, bows or other ornaments. Hang in a prominent place. Makes 1 wreath.

BE ADVENTUROUS
   Some of the recipes in this book may sound outlandish, but if you don't try them you'll never know how good they are.

Decorative Syrup-Coated Popcorn For Shapes & Sculptures

More for decoration than for eating.

2 qts. unbuttered popcorn
1 cup sugar
1/3 cup light corn syrup

1/2 cup water
Food coloring, if desired

Preheat oven to 250°F (121°C). Place popcorn in a large, 4-inch-deep, buttered baking pan and keep warm in oven. In a large saucepan, mix sugar, corn syrup and water. Cook over medium heat, stirring constantly, until mixture comes to a boil. Continue cooking until mixture reaches 265°F (129°C) on a candy thermometer. Remove from heat. If desired, add food coloring. Remove popcorn from oven. Pour syrup over popcorn. Stir with a large spoon just until the syrup is evenly distributed. Make the desired shapes or sculptures. Makes 2 quarts of syrup-coated popcorn.

COLORING SHAPES & SCULPTURES

Food coloring comes in 2 forms: liquid food coloring and paste dyes. They are both vegetable based and certified as safe to use in foods by the Food and Drug Administration.

You can buy liquid food coloring in bottled sets in the supermarket. Only a few drops will tint frosting or syrup. Because a lot of liquid food colorings is needed to achieve deep colors, you may find that after adding enough of it to reach the depth of color you want, the syrup or frosting is thinner than desired. You can compensate for the extra liquid by decreasing the amount of liquid required in the recipe by a corresponding amount.

Paste dyes are usually available in cake decorating shops or department stores. They are concentrated and come in sets of several small jars. The range of available colors is wider than with the liquid food coloring. Because paste dyes are concentrated, you need only a tiny bit on the end of a toothpick or on the point of a knife to color syrup or frosting. The color blends in very quickly. Because the dye is not a liquid and only a small amount is needed, adding it does not thin down syrup or frosting.

Whichever type of food coloring you buy, read the directions on the package carefully and follow instructions.

The Zorox Family & Poppo The Clown

The friendly Zorox family is as close as your kitchen and a panful of syrup-covered popcorn. Use any popcorn ball or sculpture recipe.

Start with 2 large popcorn balls and 2 or 3 small ones. Flatten the bottom of all the balls so they'll stand up by themselves. Press small candies into the ball to make shining eyes. Attach licorice strips, toothpicks or pipe cleaners topped with miniature marshmallows for antennas. Cut out oversized cardboard feet and press each member of the Zorox family onto his own feet.

If you want hats on your family instead of antennas, top each ball with a flat cooky. Place a marshmallow or gumdrop on top of the cooky and secure it with a toothpick. If a mouth seems necessary, add it with a bit of licorice string or small pieces of candy. For a final dramatic effect, attach a candy cane to the man of the family and a miniature paper parasol to the woman. Give each Zorox child a miniature flag or other tiny toy to carry.

To make Zorox cats, add tails and whiskers with licorice strips, toothpicks or pipecleaners.

To make Poppo the Clown, form a large popcorn ball and use frosting for the eyes, nose and mouth. Then frost an ice-cream cone, turn it upside down and place it on top of the popcorn ball. Press pieces of popcorn and small, brightly colored candy into the frosting on the hat. A paper coaster or a paper doily becomes a flouncy collar. Tack a bow over the collar with a toothpick.

Poppo the Clown and other popcorn characters make intriguing centerpieces, party favors and game prizes. Little children will love a clown or other character on a stick. Instead of cardboard feet, insert a stick or skewer into the bottom of each popcorn ball before it hardens. This makes them easy to carry and a bit neater to eat.

POPCORN-BALL WREATH

To make a popcorn-ball wreath, follow the directions for any popcorn-ball recipe in the section Balls, Bars & Crunches, pages 56 to 80. You will need 16 to 24 popcorn balls, depending on the size wreath you want. Wrap each popcorn ball in brightly colored plastic wrap. Cut a wreath-shape base out of stiff cardboard the same size you want your wreath to be. Stand the cardboard base up against the wall or a piece of furniture and work from the bottom of the wreath to the top. Using cellphane tape, attach strong thread to the plastic wrap of each ball, then tape the thread to the cardboard, making the threads as short as possible. In this way cover the cardboard with popcorn balls, fitting them together as close as possible. Trim with ribbons, candy canes, sprigs of holly or mistletoe or other decorations.

Desserts

POPCORN AS A REWARD

Rewarding children for dutifully performing chores or reaching high levels of achievement is widely debated. If you favor rewarding, why not give popcorn as a reward? Keep a supply of freshly popped popcorn in a tightly covered container so you won't have to assemble the popping equipment and ingredients every time you want to present a reward. Children are happy with buttered and salted popcorn. But an extra-special treat may be useful. Try one of the recipes in this section. Fluffy Chocolate-Chip Cookies and fresh-baked Lemon Coolers are treats your children will yearn for.

And what about you? Next time, treat yourself to a popcorn reward.

Most of the popcorn ball and popcorn crunch recipes can be made into popcorn cookies. Mix the syrup with the popped popcorn and allow it to cool slightly. Drop it by the spoonful on a buttered cooky sheet or waxed paper. If the recipe calls for mixing raisins, gumdrops or similar ingredients in with the popcorn, use them instead to decorate the tops of the cookies.

To make a cake using the recipes for popcorn balls and crunches, press the popcorn-syrup mixture into an angel-food cake pan and cool. To remove the cake, set the pan in 1 or 2 inches of water and loosen the cake from the edge of the pan with a spatula. Frost the cake with melted caramel, melted chocolate or frosting.

Popcorn sundaes are easy to make, fun for your guests and very satisfying as a dessert. Give each person an individual bowl of plain, toasted or buttered, but not salted, popped popcorn. Let your guests top their own with brown sugar, chocolate sauce, nuts, malt powder, maple syrup, molasses or whipped cream.

Although most of the recipes in this section will remain fresh and crisp for many days, some, such as Bon Bons, Popcream Delight, Popcorn Smacks and Crunchy Ice-Cream Topping, should not be prepared until just before serving. After sitting for 30 minutes covered with chocolate sauce or maple syrup, the crunchiness of the popcorn and most of the appeal of the dessert may be lost.

DESSERT SHELLS

Popcorn makes unusual and decorative dessert shells. Use the recipe for Light-Syrup Glaze or Dark-Syrup Glaze, page 142. Add food coloring to the syrup to give the shells a pretty pastel color. Working quickly, mold the warm popcorn-syrup mixture over an upside-down, buttered custard cup or other small bowl. Chill the dessert shells in the refrigerator. Fill the chilled cups with sherbert, fruit, pudding, candy or even popcorn.

To make popcorn cones, mold the warm popcorn-syrup mixture over buttered cone-shaped paper or plastic cups. Chill and fill them with ice cream or candy.

GROUND POPCORN

A few of the recipes in this section require ground popped popcorn. Grinding popcorn in a blender or food processor is quite simple. See the section on Ground Popcorn, page 96.

Crunchy Ice-Cream Topping

An economical way to glamorize ice cream.

2 tablespoons butter
3 tablespoons brown sugar

1 cup medium or finely ground,
    popped popcorn

In a small saucepan, melt butter over low heat. Sprinkle in brown sugar. Mix in ground popcorn and stir over low heat for several minutes. Pour off the excess butter, if any. Serve immediately as a topping on ice cream. Makes 4 servings.

Crunchy Bars

Popcorn gives a new taste dimension to standard flavors.

4 cups medium-ground, popped popcorn
1/2 cup brown sugar, firmly packed

1/2 cup butter
1 teaspoon cinnamon

Preheat oven to 375°F (190°C). Lightly butter an 8-inch-square baking pan. Combine ingredients and mix well. Press firmly into buttered baking pan. Bake for 15 minutes. Cut into 2" x 2" bars and let cool. Makes 16 bars.

Butterscotch Brownies

Especially good when warm.

1 cup dark-brown sugar, firmly packed
1/4 cup vegetable oil
1 egg
1/2 cup chopped nuts

1 teaspoon vanilla
3/4 cup finely ground, popped popcorn
1 teaspoon baking powder
1/2 teaspoon salt

Preheat oven to 350°F (177°C). Butter an 8-inch-square baking pan. In a large bowl, stir together brown sugar, oil and egg until smooth. Mix in nuts and vanilla. Mix together ground popcorn, baking powder and salt. Add to the oil mixture, stirring well. Spread evenly in the buttered pan. Bake for 20 minutes or until browned. Cut into squares while warm. Makes 16 brownies.

Banana Pops

Chocolate-dipped fresh fruit—crunchy, too.

2 bananas	3 tablespoons sugar
4 wooden sticks	2 tablespoons butter
2/3 cup semi-sweet cooking chips or	3 tablespoons milk
chopped milk-chocolate candy bars	2 cups medium-ground, popped popcorn

Cut the bananas in half crossways. Carefully insert wooden sticks into the cut ends of the bananas, to serve as skewers. Place on a plate in the freezer. Melt the chocolate, butter and sugar over low heat. Stir in the milk. Sprinkle with 1/4 cup of the ground popcorn. Place the remaining ground popcorn in a large bowl. Remove the chilled bananas from the freezer one at a time and hold over the pan of melted-chocolate mixture. Use a tablespoon or small ladle to drizzle the chocolate over the banana, allowing the excess to run back into the pan. Coat the chocolate-covered banana with ground popcorn, lightly pressing the popcorn into the chocolate. As each banana pop is finished place immediately on a plate in the freezer. Freeze for several hours before serving. Makes 4 banana pops.

Variations:
In place of the milk chocolate use an equal amount of chopped candy bars such as Almond Joy® or Milky Way®.

Make smaller pieces with banana chunks or whole cherries instead of banana halves

Sprinkle ground popcorn into melted chocolate mixture

Hold the banana on a stick over the chocolate pan. Spoon
the chocolate mixture over the banana, coating evenly.

Coat the chocolate-covered banana with ground popcorn.
As soon as each banana is coated, place on a plate in
the freezer.

Bon Bons

Perfect accompaniment for after-dinner coffee.

1-1/3 cups milk chocolate   1/3 cup milk
1/3 cup sugar   2 qts. medium-ground popcorn
1/4 cup butter

Lightly butter a cooky sheet. In a medium saucepan, heat the chocolate, sugar, butter and milk over low heat until melted. Pour over ground popcorn and mix well. Shape into small, 1-inch mounds. Place in freezer at least 1 hour before serving. Makes approximately 30 bon bons.

Variations:
In place of the milk chocolate use an equal amount of chopped, chocolate candy bars, or chocolate cooking pieces, and heat with other ingredients until melted.

Form the popcorn-chocolate mixture around 1/2-inch-square pieces of bananas, cherries, marshmallows or small candies.

Popcream Delight

Your children will enjoy making this creamy-fruit dessert.

1 cup raisins   1/2 cup cream or whipped cream
1 cup medium-ground popped popcorn

Soak the raisins in warm water until they are well plumped. Drain and mix with the popcorn. Chill. Serve with plain or whipped cream stirred into the mixture. Makes 4 small servings.

Variations:
Try chopped apples, chopped pineapple, nuts, sliced banana, mandarin orange slices, seedless grapes or miniature marshmallows in addition to, or substituted for, the raisins.

Zucchini Energy Bars

Good for a snack, too. Serve with cold milk or cider.

1/2 cup butter
1/2 cup vegetable oil
1 cup brown sugar, firmly packed
2 eggs
2 tablespoons water
1 teaspoon vanilla
1-1/4 cups white, enriched flour
1 teaspoon baking soda

1/2 teaspoon salt
1/2 cup whole-wheat flour
1-1/2 cups raisins
2 cups medium-ground, popped popcorn
3 cups coarsely grated zucchini
1 teaspoon cinnamon
Powdered sugar, if desired

Preheat oven to 350°F (177°C). Butter a 13" x 9" baking pan. In a large mixing bowl, beat butter, oil and brown sugar until fluffy. Beat in eggs, water and vanilla. Sift together white flour, baking soda and salt. Add to ingredients in bowl along with the whole-wheat flour. Mix until just blended. Stir in raisins, ground popcorn and zucchini. Spread in buttered pan. Sprinkle with cinnamon. Bake for 35 to 40 minutes or until wooden pick comes out clean. If desired, sprinkle with powdered sugar. Cut into bars when cool. Makes 24 bars.

Prune Pudding

Light and spicy.

1-1/3 cup dried prunes
2 cups cold water
1 cup sugar
1/3 of a cinnamon stick
1-1/3 cups boiling water

1/3 cup cornstarch
1/4 to 1/3 cup water
1 tablespoon lemon juice
2 eggs whites, stiffly beaten
1/2 cup medium-ground, popped popcorn

Soak prunes for 1 hour in 2 cups of cold water. Boil until soft. Pour water off and remove pits. Add sugar, piece of cinnamon stick and boiling water. Simmer about 10 minutes. Add cornstarch diluted in 1/4 to 1/3 cup water. Cook for 5 minutes. Remove piece of cinnamon stick. Add lemon juice, egg whites and ground popcorn. Mix well. Pour in molds and chill. Serve with plain or whipped cream. Makes 8 servings.

Variations:
Substitute apricots or other dried fruit for prunes.

Fantasy Cake

Real enough to top with birthday candles.

1 cup butter	1 cup peanuts
1 (1-lb.) bag marshmallows	1 cup M & M's®
2 qts. popped popcorn	1 cup gum drops

In a large saucepan, melt butter and marshmallows together over low heat. In a large, deep bowl, mix all other ingredients. Add the butter-marshmallow mixture. Stir well. Pack in an 8-inch-square, glass baking dish. Cool in refrigerator. Cut in 4" x 1" pieces when cool. Cut again, when cold. Makes 16 pieces.

Caramel Pie Crust

Use this crust with ice-cream filling or pre-cooked and cooled filling.

18 caramels (approximately 1 cup)	1/4 teaspoon cinnamon
2 tablespoons milk	Dash of salt
1/3 cup chopped salted peanuts	3 cups coarsely ground, popped popcorn

Lightly butter a 9-inch pie plate. Melt caramels with milk in the top of a double boiler, stirring frequently until creamy. Remove from heat and add peanuts, cinnamon and salt. Pour over popcorn and toss until all is coated. Press mixture into the buttered pie plate. Place in freezer to harden. Do not cook this crust along with the filling or use for a hot filling. Makes one 9-inch pie crust.

Jewel Cake

The calorie counter's version of Fantasy Cake.

2 qts. popped popcorn	1-1/2 tablespoons vegetable oil
3/4 cup peanuts	2 tablespoons butter
1 cup gum drops	2 cups marshmallows

Butter a 13" x 9" glass baking dish. Mix popcorn, peanuts and gum drops together in a large pan. Heat oil, butter and marshmallows together over low to medium heat until butter and marshmallows are melted. Pour over the popcorn mixture. Mix well. When popcorn is thoroughly coated, pour into buttered dish. Refrigerate. Cut when cool, again when cold. Makes 24 pieces.

Light-Syrup Glaze

Use to make colorful and spicy dessert shells.

2 cups sugar
1 cup light corn syrup

1 cup water
1/2 cup butter

Before making glaze, preheat oven to 250°F (121°C). Place popcorn to be used for shapes in a large, 4-inch-deep, buttered baking pan. Keep warm in the oven. Cook sugar, corn syrup, water and butter together until mixture reaches 260°F (127°C) on a candy thermometer. Remove popcorn from oven. Mix sugar-syrup mixture with popcorn and form into shapes while still warm. Mold into ice-cream bowls, fruit bowls or pie crusts. But don't fill the pie crusts with pie fillings containing much liquid unless the pie will be eaten immediately. Makes glaze to cover 3 to 5 quarts of popped popcorn.

Variations:
Color this glaze with food coloring, paste dyes or gelatin. If the shapes are to be eaten, flavor the glaze with spices, such as pumpkin-pie spice or cinnamon.

Dark-Syrup Glaze

Use to make old-fashioned-flavored shells to hold ice cream, fruit or pie filling.

3/4 cup molasses
1-1/2 cups light-brown sugar, firmly packed
1 tablespoon vinegar

1/2 cup butter
1/2 teaspoon salt

Before making glaze, preheat oven to 250°F (121°C). Place popcorn to be used for shapes in a large, 4-inch-deep, buttered baking pan. Keep warm in the oven. Cook molasses, brown sugar, vinegar, butter and salt together, stirring frequently, until mixture reaches 260°F (127°C) on a candy thermometer. Remove popcorn from oven and mix with glaze. Form into shapes while still warm. The uses for this glaze are similar to Light-Syrup Glaze, except it cannot be colored. Dark-Syrup Glaze has more flavor and does not need other ingredients added for flavor. Makes glaze to cover 3 to 5 quarts popped popcorn.

Variation:
Substitute 3/4 cup white sugar and 3/4 cup dark-brown sugar for light-brown sugar.

Peach-Melba Pie

Grand finale for an elegant dinner.

1 qt. peach ice cream, slightly softened
1 Brown-Sugar Crust, see page 146

1 pt. vanilla ice cream, slightly softened
1 cup peach slices

Sauce:
1 (10-oz.) pkg. thawed raspberries
1/2 cup sugar

1 tablespoon cornstarch

Spoon peach ice cream into pie crust. Place in the freezer. When frozen, spoon vanilla ice cream over the top and freeze again. Just before serving with sauce, arrange peach slices on top. Makes 1 pie.

Sauce:
Drain raspberries and save the syrup. Combine sugar and cornstarch in a saucepan. Add syrup and bring to a boil. Cook until thickened, stirring constantly. Fold in raspberries. Cool. Serve over individual pieces of pie.

Crunchy Pie Crust

Use this crust for pies requiring lengthy cooking times at high temperature.

1 cup flour
2/3 cup finely ground, popped popcorn
1/4 cup finely chopped almonds

1-1/3 tablespoons sugar
1/4 cup butter
4 tablespoons cold water

Lightly butter a 9-inch pie plate. Combine flour, ground popcorn, almonds and sugar. Mix well. Add butter and stir until the mixture is coarse and crumbly. Slowly add water, mixing just until the dry ingredients are moist enough to form a ball. On a floured surface roll the pastry out into a thin 11-inch circle. Place in pie plate and trim to 1/8-inch overhang. Makes one 9-inch pie crust.

Variation:
To make individual pies, roll pastry into 4 small circles and place each in a tart-size pan.

Pink Birthday-Party Pie

Using this as a basic recipe, you can design your own party pie.

1 qt. popped popcorn
3/4 cup granulated sugar
1/4 cup light corn syrup
1 tablespoon butter
1/4 teaspoon salt
1/8 teaspoon cream of tartar

1 to 2 tablespoons strawberry-flavored
  gelatin powder
1/2 teaspoon baking soda
1 qt. French-vanilla ice cream,
  slightly softened
Fresh strawberries, halved

Preheat oven to 200°F (93°C). Place popcorn in a large, 4-inch-deep baking pan. Keep warm in oven. Butter a 9 or 10-inch pie plate. Combine the sugar, corn syrup, butter, salt and cream of tartar in a large saucepan. Bring to a boil, stirring constantly. Cook, without stirring, until mixture reaches 250°F (121°C) on a candy thermometer. Stir in gelatin powder. Continue cooking for about 1 minute until mixture reaches 260°F (127°C). Remove from heat. Add baking soda and stir in quickly but thoroughly. Remove popcorn from oven. Immediately pour syrup mixture while foamy over popcorn. Mix gently to coat thoroughly. Press, with lightly buttered fingers, onto the bottom and sides of buttered pie plate. Bake for 45 minutes. Cool. Fill with ice cream, spreading smooth with the back of a spoon. Just before serving, arrange strawberry halves cut side down in a pattern over the top. Serve at once or keep in freezer until ready to serve. When storing pie in the freezer, do not add strawberries until just before serving. Makes 1 pie.

Variations:

To make Valentine-Party Pie, use raspberry-flavored gelatin powder and make pie shell in a buttered heart-shaped mold. When cool, fill with raspberry sherbert. Decorate with poufs of whipped cream.

To make Christmas-Party Pie, use cherry-flavored gelatin powder and make pie shell in a Christmas mold. When cool, fill with pistachio ice cream. Sprinkle with red or green cake-decorating candy crystals.

To make Halloween-Party Pie, use orange-flavored gelatin powder. When cool, fill the pie shell with chocolate ice cream. Garnish with whipped cream and sprinkle with confetti cake decorations.

Brown-Sugar Crust

Do not use this crust for pies requiring a lengthy cooking time at a high temperature.

2-1/2 cups medium-ground, popped popcorn
1/2 cup melted butter

1/4 cup brown sugar, firmly packed
1/4 teaspoon cinnamon

Lightly butter a 9-inch pie plate. Combine all ingredients. Press firmly onto the bottom and sides of the buttered pie plate.

Variation:
To make ice-cream cups, divide mixture into 4 parts and press into 4 individual tart-size pans.

Purpled Pie

For a pretty effect, match your table decorations to the pie color.

1 Caramel Pie Crust, see page 140, or
   1 Brown-Sugar Crust, see above
1 qt. ice cream or sherbet
1/2 cup grape juice

1/2 cup grape jelly
1 tablespoon cornstarch
2 tablespoons grape juice

Fill pie crust with slightly softened ice cream or sherbet, piled high in the center. Place in freezer. Combine 1/2 cup grape juice and jelly in a large saucepan. Bring to a boil. Mix cornstarch with 2 tablespoons grape juice and add to boiling liquid. Cook, stirring constantly, over medium heat until thickened. Cool syrup. Remove pie from freezer and cut into individual pieces. Pour syrup over each piece of pie. Makes 1 pie.

Variation:
To make individual pies, press pie crust into 4 tart-size pans.

Cherry-Heart Pie

If you don't have a heart-shaped pan, make a whipped-cream heart on top of the pie filling.

1 Caramel Pie Crust, see page 140, or
   1 Brown-Sugar Crust, see page 146

1 to 1-1/2 cups cherry-pie filling
Ice cream or whipped cream, if desired

Prepare pie crust in a heart-shaped pan. Spoon pie filling into crust. Cool before serving. Top with ice cream or whipped cream, if desired. Makes 1 pie.

Popcorn Smacks

Very elegant on a tea tray.

2 cups powdered sugar
2 cups finely ground, popped popcorn
4 tablespoons flour

4 egg whites
1/2 teaspoon salt

Preheat oven to 325°F (163°C). Cut brown wrapping paper to fit on cooky sheets and lightly cover paper with butter. Mix sugar, ground popcorn and flour. Beat egg whites until stiff and add salt. Gradually add the popcorn mixture to egg whites, then drop by teaspoonfuls onto buttered brown paper placed on cooky sheets. Bake for 30 minutes or until browned. Makes 2 dozen.

Raisin Fluffies

A dainty dessert served with fruit sherbert.

4 egg whites
1 cup coarsely ground, popped popcorn
1/4 cup chopped raisins

2 cups powdered sugar
2 tablespoons flour
1/4 cup shredded coconut

Preheat oven to 375°F to 400°F (190°C to 204°C). Butter cooky sheets. Beat egg whites until stiff. Fold in remaining ingredients. Drop by tablespoonfuls on buttered cooky sheets. Bake for 15 minutes or until golden brown. Makes 1-1/2 dozen.

Fruit Cookies

No cookie jar can hold these for long.

1 cup finely ground, popped popcorn
1 cup sugar
1 cup chopped dried figs, apricots or
   other dried fruit
1/2 cup vegetable shortening
1/2 cup milk

1 egg, beaten
1 cup whole-wheat flour
1 cup cornmeal
1 teaspoon salt
1-1/2 teaspoons nutmeg
4 teaspoons baking powder

Preheat oven to 350°F (177°C). Lightly butter cooky sheets. Mix together ground popcorn, sugar, dried fruit, shortening, milk and egg. Gradually add flour, cornmeal, salt, nutmeg and baking powder. Drop by tablespoonfuls on buttered cooky sheets. Flatten each with a fork dipped in flour. Bake for 15 minutes. Makes about 48 cookies.

Molasses-Fruit Cookies

An excellent lunch-box cookie.

2 cups flour
4 teaspoons baking powder
1 teaspoon salt
1-1/2 teaspoons nutmeg
1/2 cup vegetable oil
1 cup sugar

1/2 cup molasses
2 tablespoons milk
1 egg, well beaten
1 cup medium-ground, popped popcorn
1 cup chopped dried pears or
   other dried fruit

Preheat oven to 400°F (204°C). Butter cooky sheets. Combine flour, baking powder, salt and nutmeg. Set aside. Cream together oil and sugar. Add molasses, milk and egg. Gradually blend in the flour mixture. Add the ground popcorn and dried fruit, mixing thoroughly. Drop by teaspoonfuls onto buttered cooky sheets. Bake for 8 to 10 minutes. Makes 5 to 6 dozen.

Banana-Bread Cookies

A delectable blend of gentle flavors.

2-1/4 cups sifted flour
2 teaspoons baking powder
1/4 teaspoon salt
1/3 cup vegetable shortening
1/3 cup soft butter
1-1/3 cups sugar

2 eggs
1 teaspoon vanilla
1 cup mashed (approximately
   3 whole) bananas
3 cups finely ground, popped popcorn
2 teaspoons cinnamon

Preheat oven to 400°F (204°C). Butter cooky sheets. Sift together flour, baking powder and salt. Cream shortening and butter. Gradually add sugar, beating until light and fluffy. Add eggs one at a time, beating well. Stir in vanilla. Add flour mixture alternately with mashed bananas, beating smoothly after each addition. Stir the ground popcorn and cinnamon into the mixture. Drop by teaspoonfuls on buttered cooky sheets. Bake for 10 minutes. Makes 2-1/2 dozen.

Lemon Coolers

Cookies with a strong lemon flavor.

2 cups flour
2 cups finely ground, popped popcorn
1 cup brown sugar, firmly packed
1 cup granulated sugar
1/2 cup plus 2 tablespoons butter

1 teaspoon baking soda
2 teaspoons grated lemon peel
1 tablespoon lemon juice
2 eggs
1/4 cup powdered sugar

Preheat oven to 350°F (177°C). Lightly butter cooky sheets. Combine flour, ground popcorn, brown sugar, granulated sugar, butter, baking soda, lemon peel, lemon juice and eggs. Stir until well blended into a crumbly mixture. Form into 1-inch balls. Roll in powdered sugar. Place on buttered cooky sheets, 2 inches apart. Bake for 10 to 12 minutes or until brown. Makes approximately 4 dozen.

Fluffy Chocolate-Chip Cookies

An unusually light chocolate-chip cooky.

3 cups finely ground, popped popcorn
4 tablespoons soft butter
4 egg whites
1-1/3 cup sugar

1 teaspoon salt
2 teaspoons vanilla
1 cup semi-sweet chocolate cooking chips

Preheat oven to 325°F (163°C). Butter cooky sheets. Stir ground popcorn and butter together. In a large bowl, with mixer on high speed, beat egg whites until stiff. Gradually beat in sugar at low speed until the mixture is stiff and glossy. Beat in salt and vanilla. Fold in popcorn-butter mixture and chocolate cooking chips. Drop by heaping teaspoonfuls on buttered cooky sheets. Bake for 12 to 15 minutes or until firm and lightly browned. Makes about 2-1/2 dozen.

Raisin-Carrot Cookies

Tuck these in their lunch boxes. Add extras to share with a friend.

1/2 cup butter
1/2 cup vegetable oil
1 cup brown sugar, firmly packed
2 eggs
2 tablespoons water
1 teaspoon vanilla
1-1/2 cups flour

1 teaspoon baking soda
1 teaspoon nutmeg
1/2 teaspoon salt
2-1/2 cups finely ground, popped popcorn
1-1/2 cups raisins
3 cups coarsely grated, raw carrot
1/2 cup sunflower seeds

Preheat oven to 350°F (177°C). Butter cooky sheets. In a large mixing bowl, beat butter, oil and brown sugar until fluffy. Beat in eggs, water and vanilla. Sift together flour, baking soda, nutmeg and salt. Add to the ingredients in the bowl along with the ground popcorn. Mix until just blended. Stir in remaining ingredients. Drop large cookies well apart on buttered cooky sheet, using about 1/3 cup of batter for each cooky. Bake for 12 to 15 minutes. Cool on racks. Makes 2 dozen 3-inch cookies.

Maple-Syrup Cookies

Fresh-baked cookies and mugs of hot cocoa brighten a winter afternoon.

1 cup all-purpose flour
1/4 teaspoon salt
1 teaspoon baking powder
1 cup medium-ground, popped popcorn
1/2 cup chopped walnuts

1/2 cup vegetable shortening
1 egg
3/4 cup maple syrup
1/2 teaspoon vanilla

Preheat oven to 400°F (204°C). Butter cooky sheets. Into a large bowl, sift flour with salt and baking powder. Add ground popcorn and walnuts. Mix well and set aside. Cream shortening, add egg and beat until light and fluffy. Add maple syrup and vanilla. Mix well. Combine all ingredients. Drop by teaspoonfuls onto the buttered cooky sheets. Bake for 8 to 12 minutes. Makes 6 dozen.

Valentine Hearts

Handsome hearts for special occasions.

3 qts. popped popcorn
6 tablespoons butter
9 cups miniature marshmallows (1-1/2 pkgs.)

1/2 cup red cinnamon candies
Red cinnamon candies for decoration

Preheat oven to 250°F (121°C). Place popcorn in a large, 4-inch deep, buttered baking pan. Keep warm in oven. Butter a 6-cup heart-shaped cake pan and six 1/2-cup heart-shaped pans. In a large saucepan, melt butter over low heat. Stir in marshmallows and 1/2 cup candies until they are melted —it may take a while for the candies to melt. Remove popcorn from oven. Pour butter mixture over popcorn, stirring to coat evenly. Pack 2/3 of the popcorn mixture into the large pan and the remainder into the small pans. Chill. To remove the cake from the pan, place the pan in a shallow dish of warm water and loosen the edges of the cake from the pan with a spatula. Use the cinnamon candies for decoration. Makes 1 large heart and 6 small hearts.

Pineapple-Carrot Cake

A rich, dark cake loaded with fruit and nuts.

2 cups sugar
1-1/2 cups vegetable oil
4 eggs
2 cups flour
2 teaspoons salt
2 teaspoons cinnamon

2 teaspoons baking soda
3 cups grated carrots
1/4 cup chopped nuts
1 cup medium-ground popped popcorn
1 cup crushed pineapple, drained
1/2 cup raisins

Icing:

1 (8-oz.) pkg. cream cheese
1/2 cup butter
1 (1-lb.) box powdered sugar

2 teaspoons vanilla
1/4 cup chopped nuts

Preheat oven to 350°F (177°C). Butter and flour an 8-inch-square baking pan. In a large bowl, blend sugar and oil together. Beat eggs, then add to the sugar-oil mixture. Add remaining ingredients and blend well. Pour into greased and floured pan. Bake for 50 to 60 minutes. Let cool before icing. Makes 1 cake.

Icing:

Allow cream cheese and butter to soften at room temperature. Blend cream cheese, powdered sugar, butter and vanilla together. Spread on cooled cake. Sprinkle chopped nuts on top. Makes icing to frost 1 cake.

Chocolate Pie

Would you believe the foundation is popcorn?

1 Caramel Pie Crust, see page 140, or
   1 Brown-Sugar Crust, see page 146

1 (6-oz.) pkg. chocolate-pie filling
Whipped cream

Prepare pie filling according to the package directions. Spoon into pie shell and chill. Garnish with whipped cream just before serving. Makes 1 pie.

Variation:
Use any other flavor pudding and pie filling.

Lemon-Cheese Pie

Rich, but refreshing.

1 Brown-Sugar Crust, see page 146
2 (3-3/4-oz.) pkgs. instant lemon-pudding mix
3 cups milk
1 cup cottage cheese

2 tablespoons grated lemon peel
1/2 cup lemon juice
1/2 cup sour cream
Lemon slices for garnish

Prepare lemon pudding as directed on package, except use a total of 3 cups of milk. Beat cottage cheese with mixer on high speed until almost smooth. Blend whipped cottage cheese, grated lemon peel and lemon juice into the pudding. Mix well. Spoon into pie crust. Top with sour cream and chill. Garnish with lemon slices. Makes 1 pie.

Special thanks to: William Smith, Mary Margaret Carberry, Pat O'Keefe and Shelia Sandy of The Popcorn Institute; Wrede Smith, Garrett Smith, Carlton Smith, John Hassebroek and Shelby Johnstone, Jr. of The American Popcorn Company; Orville Redenbacher; Al Tunick and Kenneth Jones of Karmelkorn® Shoppes, Rock Island, Illinois; Robert and Claudia Wells of the Berkshire County Savings Bank; Don Mader of Karmelkorn® Shoppes, Glendale, Arizona; Charles Cretors; Ray M. Lien of Purdue University; Wyandot Popcorn Company; Weaver Popcorn Company; Hunt-Wesson Foods; Fun Foods; Pearson and Company; Mall Concessions, Christown, Phoenix, Arizona, Opryland, U.S.A.®; Cracker Jack Company; Craven Foundation; Odell Concession Specialties; Concession Foods, Phoenix, Arizona; Double D Foods; LuAnna Foods; National Oats Company; Purity Mills; Consolidated Popcorn; Quinn Popcorn; TNT Food Products; Mr. and Mrs. Emery Brinkman; RWB; and Ron Dobbins, researcher. Table Talk of Tucson furnished props for photographs.

THE POPCORN INSTITUTE

The Popcorn Institute, headquartered in Chicago, is an association representing most of the companies engaged in popcorn processing. Its purpose is to promote consumer education, product research and development, and to encourage the consumption of popcorn. The Institute frequently develops new recipes for using popcorn and makes them available to newspapers across the country. Many of the recipes in this book were originally developed by the Institute, and others are variations of their ideas.

POPPING JARGON

Old Maids—Some kernels remain unpopped at the bottom of the popper. They are called *old maids* or *grannies.* Old maids call them grannies. Grannies call them old maids. Proper popping should reduce their number to as little as 1% of the number of kernels popped. It is usually not worth the trouble to attempt to re-pop old maids.

Pearls and Rice—There are 2 basic shapes of kernels. Pearls are short and thick with round crowns. Rice kernels are long and slender with a pointed crown sometimes ending in a hook or beak.

Mushrooms and Butterflies—These terms describe the shapes of popped popcorn pieces. Mushrooms are almost round and are sometimes called cauliflowers. Butterflies are irregular, branched and pronged and are preferred by people who sell popped corn to the public.

Mushrooms are tougher and are preferred by makers of popcorn balls and caramel corn because they don't break easily. The ratio of mushrooms to butterflies depends on the type of popcorn, although some experts suggest that excessive heat can increase the number of mushrooms.

Bee's Wings—The tiny flecks that stick to the sides and bottom of packages of unpopped popcorn come from the very tip of the kernel where it was attached to the ear. Most of the bee's wings are removed at the factory, but a few still cling to the kernels and end up in the package. They have no important dietary, social, or economic significance. Not even to bees.

Index

CONVERSION TO METRIC MEASURE

WHEN YOU KNOW	SYMBOL	MULTIPLY BY	TO FIND	SYMBOL
teaspoons	tsp	5	milliliters	ml
tablespoons	tbsp	15	milliliters	ml
fluid ounces	fl oz	30	milliliters	ml
cups	c	0.24	liters	l
pints	pt	0.47	liters	l
quarts	qt	0.95	liters	1
ounces	oz	28	grams	g
pounds	lb	0.45	kilograms	kg
Fahrenheit	°F	5/9 (after subtracting 32)	Celsius	C
inches	in	2.54	centimeters	cm
feet	ft	30.5	centimeters	cm

LIQUID MEASURE TO MILLILITERS

1/4 teaspoon	=	1.25 milliliters
1/2 teaspoon	=	2.5 milliliters
3/4 teaspoon	=	3.75 milliliters
1 teaspoon	=	5 milliliters
1-1/4 teaspoons	=	6.25 milliliters
1-1/2 teaspoons	=	7.5 milliliters
1-3/4 teaspoons	=	8.75 milliliters
2 teaspoons	=	10 milliliters
1 tablespoon	=	15 milliliters
2 tablespoons	=	30 milliliters

LIQUID MEASURE TO LITERS

1/4 cup	=	0.06 liters
1/2 cup	=	0.12 liters
3/4 cup	=	0.18 liters
1 cup	=	0.24 liters
1-1/4 cups	=	0.3 liters
1-1/2 cups	=	0.36 liters
2 cups	=	0.48 liters
2-1/2 cups	=	0.6 liters
3 cups	=	0.72 liters
3-1/2 cups	=	0.84 liters
4 cups	=	0.96 liters
4-1/2 cups	=	1.08 liters
5 cups	=	1.2 liters
5-1/2 cups	=	1.32 liters

FAHRENHEIT TO CELSIUS

F	C
200°	93°
225°	107°
250°	121°
275°	135°
300°	149°
325°	163°
350°	177°
375°	191°
400°	205°
425°	218°
450°	232°
475°	246°
500°	260°

SPICE CHART

NAME AND DESCRIPTION	COMPATIBLE WITH:

Allspice
    Color—brown
    Flavor—spicy, sweet, mild, pleasant
	All cranberry dishes, spice cakes, beef stew, baked ham, mincemeat and pumpkin pie, tapioca & chocolate pudding

Anise
    Color—brown with tan stripes
    Flavor—sweet licorice aroma and taste
	Coffee cake, rolls, cookies, all fruit pie fillings, sweet pickles, stewed fruits

Basil
    Color—light green
    Flavor—mild, sweet
	All tomato dishes, green vegetables, stews, shrimp and lobster dishes

Bay Leaves
    Color—light green
    Flavor—very mild, sweet
	Vegetables, stews, shrimp, lobster, chicken dishes, pot roasts

Caraway
    Color—dark brown with light brown stripes
    Flavor—like rye bread
	Cheese spreads, breads and rolls, cookies, vegetables, roast pork

Cardamom
    Color—cream-colored pod, dark brown seeds
    Flavor—bitter-sweet
	Danish pastry, coffee cake, custards, sweet potato and pumpkin dishes

Cayenne
    Color—burnt orange
    Flavor—hot
	Deviled eggs, fish dishes, cooked green vegetables, cheese souffles, pork chops, veal stew

Celery Seed
    Color—shades of brownish green
    Flavor—bitter celery
	Meat loaf, fish chowders, cole slaw, stewed tomatoes, rolls, salad dressings

Chili Powder
    Color—light to dark red
    Flavor—distinctive, hot
	Mexican cookery, chili, beef, pork and veal dishes, Spanish rice

Cinnamon
    Color—light brown
    Flavor—sweet and spicy
	Coffee cakes, spice cake, cookies, puddings, fruit pies, spiced beverages, sweet potato and pumpkin dishes

Cloves
    Color—dark brown
    Flavor—spicy, sweet, pungent
	Ham, apple, mince & pumpkin pies, baked beans, hot tea, spice cake, puddings, cream of pea and tomato soups

Cumin
    Color—gold with a hint of green
    Flavor—salty sweet
	Deviled eggs, chili, rice, fish

Curry Powder
    Color—Predominantly rich gold
    Flavor—exotic with heat
	Eggs, fish, poultry, creamed vegetables, chowders, tomato soup, salted nuts

Dill
    Color—greenish brown
    Flavor—similar to caraway, but milder and sweeter
	Pickling, potato salad, soups, vegetables, salad dressing, drawn butter for shellfish

Ginger
    Color—tan
    Flavor—spicy
	Cookies, spice cake, pumpkin pie, puddings, applesauce, stews, French dressing

Mace
    Color—burnt orange
    Flavor—similar to nutmeg, exotic
	Fish, stews, pickling, gingerbread, cakes. Welsh rarebit, chocolate dishes, fruit pies

Marjoram
    Color—green
    Flavor—delicate
	Lamb chops, roast beef, poultry, omelets, stews, stuffings

Mint
    Color—green
    Flavor—sweet
	Jelly, fruit salad, lamb and veal roast, tea

Mustard
    Color—light to dark brown
    Flavor—spicy, sharp
	Pickling, Chinese hot sauce, cheese sauce, vegetables, molasses cookies

Nutmeg
    Color—copper
    Flavor—exotic, sweet
	Doughnuts, eggnog, custards, spice cake, coffee cake, pumpkin pie, sweet potatoes

Oregano
    Color—green
    Flavor—strong
	Pizza, spaghetti sauce, meat sauces, soups, vegetables

Paprika
    Color—red
    Flavor—very mild
	Poultry, goulash, vegetables, canapes, chowders

Parsley
    Color—green
    Flavor—mild
	Soups, salads, meat stews, all vegetables, potatoes

Pepper
    Color—black or white
    Flavor—spicy, enduring aftertaste
	Almost all foods except those with sweet flavors. Use white pepper when black specks are not desired.

Poppy Seeds
    Color—blue-gray
    Flavor—crunchy, nutlike
	Breads and rolls, salad dressings, green peas

Rosemary
    Color—green
    Flavor—delicate, sweetish
	Lamb, beef, pork, poultry, soups, cheese sauces, potatoes

Saffron
    Color—red-orange
    Flavor—exotic
	Rice, breads, fish stew, chicken soup, cakes

Savory
    Color—green
    Flavor—mild, pleasant
	Scrambled eggs, poultry stuffing, hamburgers, fish, tossed salad

Sesame Seeds
    Color—cream
    Flavor—crunchy, nutlike
	Breads and rolls, cookies, salad dressings, fish, asparagus

Tarragon
    Color—green
    Flavor—fresh, pleasant
	Marinades of meat, poultry, omelets, fish, soups, vegetables

Thyme
    Color—olive green
    Flavor—pleasantly penetrating
	Tomato dishes, fish chowder, all meats, potatoes

Turmeric
    Color—orange
    Flavor—mild, slightly bitter
	Pickles, salad dressings, seafood, rice